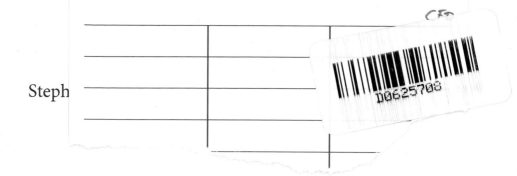

Steph

# Divine

# Emanations

Various Messages III

Divine Emanations- Various Messages III © 2013 Stephan Attia

**ISBN: 978-1-494-26130-6**

# Preface:

Unlike my other books that deal with divine messages, I have decided that in this book I shall comment on each message at the same chapter. The following divine messages were written down as notes on paper during the last few years. I had not the time to work on them beforehand, thus I have always felt that their incompletion was breathing down my neck each time I was working on other books. After I have published 'The Balance of Justice' and 'The Library of Time' I have experienced a great catharsis that reminded me about this cluster of unpublished messages. The divine messages, however, are associated with other books which I have written throughout the years. For me, living in exile was an epic journey because I have sojourned in the divine realism despite of all the tumults and social upheavals of my age. It felt really strange for me to cope with every day's life in a human realism which was very alien to me. In consciousness I was often elsewhere and had a horrible time to try and survive the physical reality. I did not pay much attention to the survival mentality, which was a super flock mentality associated with Darwinism and subsequently with primitivism. For me equality was a natural virtue, or a simple principle, which I have deemed as a simple fact. However, when I have discovered, to my horror that the vast majority of Occidental society perceived equality as a myth I was stricken with the corollary of deep pain of betrayal. Selfishness was the chief hallmark of survival among the survivalists of my age. In my skepticism I have found myself rebelling against survival. Vanity for me was the most boring thing in the world, thus I dismissed selfishness, because I have found it much more fascinating to follow the core of the truth of evolution. For me, literature in general, and poetry in particular, were the real progress in life. It is by a streak of luck, I feel, that I have survived such a selfish generation. My loyalty to fairness and equality was equated with my devotion to love and peace, and with my admiration towards life and its beauty. Thus, I have found myself in a situation when I was pushed to the edges of modern society, because of my loyalty and devotion to the divine principles of life. However, I do not regret my sufferings, because my concern was for the wholeness. I was more concerned about the earth and its species than I was concerned about my own survival. We are all part of the earth. Any tree that is cut down in a remote forest is part of our eco system. We must protect the earth before it is too late. Therefore I felt that the urgency of publishing these messages was incumbent upon me as an artist. For the cure for the earth is a healthy mankind. The purification of mankind was the key as for the healing of the earth. We have only one earth, therefore we must protect it from harm. As it is now, the earth's worst enemy is the selfishness of mankind. The madness of mankind's selfishness is based on the jungle law. We must first vanquish inequality before we can defeat selfishness. It is a long journey and hard a task, however, I believe that in the long end, we can heal the earth and restore it to its original beauty. Let's do it, doves.

Carpe Diem,

Stephan

# Contents:

## Divine Emanations

# Divine Emanations

Emanation I:     Pregnancy and birth in salvation

Dear friends, Greetings. Many people wish to be born in salvation. It is natural for one to seek happiness in life. But salvation is not religious, it is spiritual. Salvation cannot be religious because salvation is free, unbound, unfathomed, pure, and true. Salvation is love, and it cannot be put into frames. Salvation cannot be fully defined by any ideology; therefore salvation can only come from a good heart, from art. Thus, salvation can come from moral virtue and from the principle of creativity. But salvation can never come from power or from bigotry. Moreover, before a person can be born in salvation, one has to conceive the seed of salvation. The seed of salvation is the spiritual gift of the individual soul. Such a seed can also be described as a divine contract, or as a divine call. In other words, the divine seed of salvation is the inner true vocation. It is an individual seed that can grow and become a luxuriant tall tree. However, pregnancy in salvation occurs when the seed of divine law is conceived, thereupon adapted by the heart of the individual. Thus, divine knowledge is adapted by the heart as the core of faith, equality, and fairness. Thus, when a human being accepts the divine seed, there is a chance for salvation to become a reality in one's life. It is not sufficient, however, to conceive the divine seed. Pregnancy in salvation entails hard work. The duties incumbent upon a person, after accepting the divine seed, include the creation of a perfect climate, in which the seed would be able to prosper and grow. The birth in salvation takes place when a man yield fruits from the divine seed. In other words, the birth in salvation is the harvest that leads to attainment and contentment. However, before the seed of salvation can be planted, one has to be aware of it in order to accept it. For if one is not aware of the seed of salvation, then there is a big chance that the seed of salvation will be lost. There is the wind and the birds that could drag it and snap it away from one. Therefore we should always search for the truth of our existence on earth. For when we find the divine seed of salvation, we are already half way to the harvest. Thenceforth, it is a matter of free will that determines the success of the seed's growth.

Comments:

My personal example was with poetry and literature. The discovery of the gift of poetry for me was the realization of the existence of salvation. The spiritual gift is often hidden and cannot be discovered by logic or rationality. It is intuition, emotions, and impulse that draw one closer to the truth of one's goal and dream in life. The passion and the excitement of an astronomer who sets his eyes for the stars, or the passion of an anthropologist who seeks clues underground as for the evolution of mankind, are the strong indications as for the divine seed. I had the same passion for poetry and literature, although I have only really discovered it when I was about twenty two years old. If I turned down my spiritual gift it would be equated with an abortion of a divine baby. This way I would have never found happiness and completion. If I had turned down my poetry I would have surely sentenced myself to a long perdition of frustrations. Thereupon salvation would have never dwelt within me. But because I have accepted the divine seed, after I was aware of it, that I have evolved spiritually. There are two ways to have an abortion of the divine seed that we should be warned about. The first way to have an abortion is by an individual choice, hence when one chooses to neglect one's spiritual gift; as an example, when a musician neglect his music, or when a dancer neglect his dancing. The second way to have an abortion of the divine seed is when society murders the divine seed. This happens by oppression of human rights by society. Here when one is deprived of the opportunity to evolve spiritually, or when one is deprived of the climates to evolve spiritually. In such a case the individual is forced to choose between the divine seed and the demands of society. On my personal account I have been deprived of the freedom of expression and therefore started a revolution against the spiritual dark forces which ruled world society during my lifetime on earth. Thus, oppression of human rights was the source of many

8

divine abortions. Many people were prohibited from finding happiness because of the rule of vanity which was dictated by the general mass. Dictatorship turned millions of people sad and depressed because of the oppression of the divine need to evolve spiritually. As for the self destruction of evolution I believe that many people dismiss their spiritual gifts because of impatience, despair, and other negative reasons. But the worst that a human being can experience is that when one's free will is stolen by the madness of the collective. Despite my hardships in life, after the harvest I was acting wholeheartedly on the values of divine law and equality. Therefore salvation for me became a source of healing and a liberator. There is another wonderful process which takes place during the growth of the divine seed, as here one is getting rid of the mantle of selfishness until one is born completely in altruism. Hence, one overcomes inequality and embraces equality. I remember my rebellion against selfishness and against inequality at the time I have harvested in literature. It was a success because I rebelled against selfishness through faith and deeds. First I devoted myself for helping the weak in society, thereupon I promoted other poets before myself, and the reward of doing good to others and giving was simply purifying. I have felt the catharsis that came from the gratification of the divine need to help others. When a man turns from a selfish serpent to an altruist dove of peace, then a man is born in salvation, and the reward of feeling good is matching the spiritual progress. Only then that evolution really occurs and when nirvana is felt in its wholeness. Therefore, the guidance here is to: 1- Believe in the divine seed. 2- Seek the divine seed until you find it. 3- Accept the divine seed. 4- Nurture the divine seed. 5- Give birth to the divine seed and let it grow. 6- Harvest the divine seed. 7- Cherish the divine seed and evolve with it. In case society oppresses you, I suggest that you rebel against society until you win your freedom to evolve spiritually.

Emanation II:    Transformation to vanity


Often one wonders about the difference between a fruitful life and
vanity. We know that vanity is the epitome of self destruction. Vanity
means spiritual death and futility. Vanity is like a black hole in space
that consumes all planets and decimates all matter. Therefore, we
should always be aware of the dangers of vanity. The affects of vanity
on our lives is detrimental and it can become devastating if we do not
intervene. The divine intervention, however, is, in fact the individual's
intervention in accordance with ethics. In order to combat vanity
within us, or within society, and subsequently defeat it, we need to be
aware of the transformation to vanity. When we think about all the
things that give our body pleasure, we should note that the abuse of
such pleasures breaks the balance of peace. When does food become
vanity? Surely not when a man consumes it and enjoys it. For it is
natural to be satisfied with food. However, when a man begins to
worship food, and subsequently becomes obsessed with it, that the
transformation to vanity occurs. It is rather the attachment to
material things that causes one to lose the balance of reason. Madness
is the outcome of obsession. In the unseen spiritual realm we build
our temples. The most widespread classical example of an infatuation
with a physical pleasure is revolving around sex. The taboos,
ceremonies and rituals around sex in modern societies have only
alienated sex and made it a myth. The obsession with sex is the
epitome of human imbalance, but not in regard to the natural urge of
sex. The transformation to vanity around sex occurs when the mind
and the heart of a human being are obsessed with sex, not the body.
Unlike the natural body's need for sex, the mind and the heart become
corrupt because of their obsession with sexual pleasure. Sex should
not be revered to a point of alienation. The worship of sex is the cause
of alienating it. Furthermore, there is a lot of mockery involved which
adds to the ceremony of worshipping physical pleasures. Thus, a filthy

secretive industry is born out of worship and mockery. It is the core of vanity to make sex unattainable. The obsessive attachment to the extremes of pleasures through drugs, sex, and alcohol is the source and reason for the transformation into vanity. Remember, doves, the mundane world is illusive. It is a deception to believe that one can find happiness in the madness of physical pleasures. Indeed, physical pleasures should not be restricted, but on the other hand, when physical pleasures are worshipped, then one in fact abuses them and prohibits one's own evolution. Abuse and destructions are the hallmarks of vanity, thus, a man cannot find contentment in the madness of physical pleasures. It is the worship of physical pleasures that transforms one to vanity. The magnetic field of the black hole is spinning rapidly like a vortex that consumes everything. But in order to avoid vanity, one has to resist it, not join it. It means that we should erect our inner temples in the spiritual realm on the foundations of salvation. When we look at nature and at the perfect balance of the eco system, we learn that the earth has the mechanism to preserve the magic of life. Therefore, we should conform to mother earth instead of destroying her. We should follow the balance of life in accordance with the cosmic energy that is bestowed upon us. Our life on earth was created out of salvation, not out of vanity. Therefore, we should ruin the temples of vanity and restore the temples of salvation. Let our hearts worship love, peace, and harmony. Let our wishes be heard in the temples of equality, fairness, and justice. Let freedom be our bible, not prejudice. Therefore, each time we put our faith in something, we should question our motives. We should always discern whether we act in accordance with salvation or not. If our hearts do not worship in the temples of salvation, then we are doomed to fade away with vanity. Every human being has the choice to be either a black hole, or a new shining star. The creation of life and the protection of it all come from the balance of salvation. The destruction of life comes from vanity. Therefore, we should not worship food, sex, money, possessions, or anything that is associated with the temple of vanity.

Material comfort is merely an illusion of happiness, for true happiness can only come from beauty and not from power. Beauty is the reflection of salvation, and it includes equality, freedom, love, peace, fairness, and altruism. All human beings are born selfish in body, but not at heart. A human being is impelled to opt at heart, whether to follow selfishness or altruism. Vanity is the temple of the selfish at heart. Salvation is the temple of the altruist. Let every human being choose a shrine. One cannot worship both vanity and salvation, for destruction and creation are not compatible.

Comments:

I felt that my digressive diction in this emanation was rather of an advantage because the transformation to vanity is associated with many other divine messages. The faith that we have in things determines who we are as individuals. Are we sheep? are we wolves? It all comes down to our worships and deeds. It is the same with survival and with the faith of the survivalist. Many people are deceiving themselves to believe that survival in a mad world is the right thing to do. For many years I have been misled by the propaganda of the collective, as here I was brainwashed to think that survival is the true purpose of human existence. By following the general mass, I, as a matter of fact, experienced a transformation to vanity. Nevertheless, the general mass accepted the destruction of the earth as a natural practice, but I never agreed to it. For me, deep inside me, despite many years of being subjected to modern slavery, conformism to an ideology of destruction was impossibility. I refused to rape the earth; I refused to become selfish and conform to a world which was based on inequality. Survival, hence, became, in fact, a destruction of all beauty. The murder of the earth and the elimination of salvation became the constitution of the realists and survivalists. Therefore, I resorted to art in order to save the earth. My rebellion against the general mass began when I realized that survival is the fine line between destruction and creativity, and that it is up to the individual to interpret the motives of society. Some agree to buy eggs of chickens that are kept in small cages all day. For such people, survivals mean to buy the cheapest eggs in the supermarket. I refused to believe in it, and only bought eggs that came out from free range chickens. The vanity of survivals was a matter of choice. The general mass always worshipped the rich and famous in society. The rabble admires the strong, the way wolves admire the alpha leader of the pack. It was the jungle law that the rabble followed. Thus, vanity ruled society, because vanity is the source of the jungle law. But unlike the general mass, I was not rejoicing with the mocking rich. My ears were attuned to the cries and whimpers of the weak in society. I sought fairness and equality, not power. I rebelled against power and against the madness of the general mass. My shrine was art, my bible was literature. My holy concubine was poetry. Thus, I was aware of the real reality, which is the spiritual realm, thus, I chose to belong to the polarity of salvation. This emanation made me think about horns and devil's tail which appear in people after they cheat one another. The jungle law has become a poplar sport, in which realists and survivalists proudly declared themselves predatory and opportunists. The power of riches allowed crime to thrive. This message also reminded me about intimate relationships. It has always been a mystery to me why folks lived by the deception that they had the right to own one another. Apart from the bond of love, I thought it was quite strange that many people lived together because they felt that they either owned their partner, or that they were owned by their partner. The pretext of marriage or intimate relationship created an obsession which broke the balance of free will. It becomes worse, as the law, not only equity, was involved in such madness. Marriage has become another vain industry. The world of man was very primitive because of vanity. The inspiration to this emanation, moreover, brought me back to the issue of survivals. An old Danish man once asked me whether I could live from my poetry. The word 'live' meant survive in the physical world because this is the only world that mankind could see. The sheer absurdity is that it is the complete opposite. Realism is a relative term. It is an optical deception. I told him that I cannot get money for my poetry and that it was never my intention to seek bread for my poetry. However, my poetry was really my spiritual bread, and without it I could not evolve in this life. Poetry was my salvation, my bride, and my rescue. In fact, without poetry I would have never survived the spiritual world. The physical world does not appeal to me because it is only temporary. But the spirit is eternal and therefore I chose not to starve it. Otherwise, I would have remained undernourished in the true world. There is a progress in the spirit. There is an evolution which the general mass chose to ignore because of the priorities of the jungle law. In this emanation the chief lesson is that one should not worship food, or money, or sex. Yes the body needs food and sex. But if the soul worships the needs a man, then one becomes corrupt in spirit. In order to maintain a pure spirit one has to stay away from temptations. Love of food, gluttony, or obsession with sex, are temptations. There is nothing wrong with food and sex, but the abuse around them is the cause of destruction.

## Emanation III:  The power of love

Greetings, dear friends. Do not underestimate the power of love, because love is destiny, and no one can defeat karma law. All human beings are born out of a reason and for a reason. All divine reasons emanate from the power of love. As human beings we are forced to opt between love and power. However, it is a fact that there is no love in power whereas there is power in love. In fact, love is the highest power and the highest law. Love is divine law. Love is the source and the force of salvation. Power is the outcome of war, but love is the emissary and servant of peace. Dear friends, do not be deceived to think that a human being is born without a reason. Such a dark thought is misleading, for it stems from vanity. All human beings have a purpose, a goal, a mission. We were born to complete something important in life, and/or to help others to complete something important in life. That something is a secret contract which can be discovered individually. Love is a liberating power, healing, amending, and completing. Therefore, we should always prioritize love and promote love in society when it is either affordable or possible. Evolution cannot be forces on society, for evolution is like a delicate flower that requires perfect conditions through which to grow and bloom. Friends, be wise shepherds, do not give wolves flowers, and do not play the flute for them. Keep love to the sheep and discern. The most beautiful things in life stem from love, so give your love freely to those who deserve it and don't waste it on those whom are not evolved enough to fathom love. A wise man does not grow an apple tree in the desert. Love needs the perfect climate in which to grow, and that place is in the heart of the righteous. Dear friends, do not cheat anyone, and do not hurt anyone. Treat all human beings equally and help those who are in need and trouble. Love is the supreme power and supreme law. Follow love and you will find the lush meadows of salvation. Promote love and you will be rewarded with the grand prizes of evolution. Worship morality and love and you will be granted with a divine happiness. Drink salvation, which is the wine of saints, and you'll be intoxicated with the purity of everlasting life.

Comments:

As this message suggests, I wish to stress here that love should not be distributed blindly in all situations. Such an instruction must be imparted here because of the dangers of the physical reality. As a principle, love should be given freely to everyone and without discrimination. However, unlike other laws, divine law is not without exceptions. It would not be pragmatic to put a flower on a gun that is aimed upon one's head. It is not enough for a man to have the best of motives and love in his heart. A man has to preserve life, cherish it, and survive it. A man should not be a pacifist, but rather a peace lover. Unlike a peace lover, the pacifist is an extremist and irrational. Pragmatism should not be ignored because of the principles of divine law. The pride of the pacifist stands against reason and pragmatism. Hence, the pacifist is a follower of madness, whereas the lover of peace is a follower of reason. Divine law is not blind. Divine law is not harsh. Divine law is neither mad nor cold. In fact, because of its vast range of exceptions the power of divine law is superior to the power of the jungle law. I only follow love when I can afford it. I am one with love as a matter of principle. I prefer art on power. But as the message suggests it would be foolish for a shepherd to play his best melodies for a pack of wolves. Indeed there is nothing like music that appeases the beast, but that is not the point here. Evolution demands a compromise, an arbitrary, a mediator, etc. It means that one can play music to the beast, providing that the beast does not devour the music player afterwards. There has to be an agreement and a guarantee that the seeds of love are not wasted in the wilderness. Every successful divine businessman knows that there has to be a mutual benefit in everything one is dealing with in life. One has to build a small garden for the seeds of love, and follow their progress and growth. One has to create the climates for love; now that is the point. And if one cannot afford it because of the madness of the physical world, one should still preserve the seeds of love in a safe place until an opportunity to evolve in love is given. The aspiration towards love is like a flame that must never be extinguished. A human being has a wonderful gift called free will. Thus, no one else can turn off the flame of love except for the individual. Therefore, it is a personal choice that must be enhanced in order to save one from self destruction. Many innocent and peace loving people went to war, because war was imposed on them. But their victory is not in survival, but rather in the choice to keep the flame of love burning. Love means also peace and equality; hence altruism is the virtue of the power of love. A true altruist is a man who believes in fairness and equality.

Emanation IV:     The parable of the lion and deer


Dear friends, greetings. It seems as if everybody is so busy to survive that no one really wants to live life to the full. It has become a drift of collective consciousness to think that life has no other meaning than a bodily survival. Many people forgot about love and many others also forgot how to live in peace. Many people forgot about the truth of their own purpose, and about the spiritual evolution. When a man doesn't know how to live his life in accordance with the truth of his birth on earth he becomes lost. Such a man is following the currents of vanity and salvation is therefore hidden from him. Many lost people just want to strike rich quickly and thrive on their fortunes without any desire to evolve spiritually. Many lost people just want to be the queen of the bees, whereas very few people wish to follow their true vocations in life and toil as bees. I tell you the truth, for universal law is firm here; any person who wishes to become the queen of the bees, is, in fact, by free will, a wasp. Material comfort is the temple of the opportunistic predator, but the spiritual gift is the temple of light for the humanistic altruist. It is by an inner choice of heart that a man chooses whether to become a bee or a wasp. The world of vanity is a world of chaos which is based on power, fears, greed, and worries. But the world of salvation is a world of divine order which is based on beauty, love, fairness, and equality. It is the survivalists, realists, and opportunists which contribute to the madness of the system of man. The establishment of mankind has betrayed the divine order and twisted the truth. The norms of mankind are based on the jungle law, because of a collective negative choice to follow power and war. One lion has hunted a heavy deer, thereupon it feasted on it. At that moment the lion is admired by endless of scavengers. It is the same with a man who strike rich in society. Such a man is suddenly admired because of the abundance of his possessions, but not because of his merits. In the lottery system everybody runs after the jackpot.

The players, in fact, run after the vanity of power. But imagine the lottery players as deer, and the jackpot as the lion. Every now and then the lion catches a deer and devours it. But the deer is transforming, because spiritual death now takes over it, and supplies it with the illusion of life. A man dies inside him when he is attracted to power. It is a strange phenomenon because of the ethical ignorance involved. Most people overlook the point of equality here. The other deer came begging before the lion so that it would consume them also. 'Devour me, no devour me' they pushed themselves before the lion. But the lion roared and told the deer that it can only eat one deer a day, and that they will have to take a number and wait for other days. 'Perhaps you will get fortunate some day' he told them and yawned. Moreover, the lion refused to eat deer that did not run away because it needed to practice its hunting skills, as it was a part of its evolution. 'Every now and then I will choose one of you by surprise, not like this, for it is unnatural' it told the deer that stood in line to be devoured. It is the same with the lottery, once a week there is a winner, but is it the right path to choose? Only a fool believes that the way to happiness is through money and power. True happiness has got nothing to do with the conditions of the physical reality. True happiness can only occur due to the fulfillment of one's true vocation in life, for the true vocation emanates from the springs of salvation.

Comments:

The messages in this emanation are ambivalent. On one hand the message here is that in this time a deer could have enjoyed life instead of waiting for a lion to consume it, because it thinks that being hunted by a lion is the goal in life. The stupidity of the deer prohibits it from evolution. It could graze and live happily without worries, but the deer were depressed and lost. The deer is in fact brainwashed to be consumed by the lion. They just lied down all of their lives and waited for the lions to eat them. Every now and then a lion came by and ate some of the deer, but most of the deer wasted their lives on the vanity of being consumed by vanity. The criticism here is chiefly against the people who waste their lives on waiting for big money to come their way. The lost and desperate only focus on material comfort, mammon, possessions, and on other vanities. By focusing on vanities folks kill their inner truth, and extinguish the flame of salvation within them. The violent predatory drift of human society made people waste their life on false hopes, despair, and futility. I have felt that it was so wrong for a human being to believe in the brainwash of the jungle law super organism. Survival has become an industry, and opportunism a religion. The ignorant is a survivalist, but the sly is an opportunist, yet both of them lead to self destruction, because both of them follow the vortex of vanity. On the other hand, the message here is to rebel against inequality, which is so widespread in human society. The heroes of a society and the zeros of a society are classified as such by the mad criteria of the jungle law constitution and spirit. Inequality is the source of such madness. The rabble despises the poor but admires and idolizes the rich. Society loves and cherishes the strong but oppresses and crushes the weak. The pack order of wild dogs, the jungle law, has taken over human societies, and now we hear about the vain private life of rich people, whereas the misery of myriads of poor people is muffled and marginalized. The incorporated media is ruled by the jungle law super organism; hence the brainwash of a mass population is taking place on a daily basis. In the modern world a child is taught that becoming rich is the right thing to do. This repeating propaganda by society is the source of the destruction of a human being. In this divine emanation the dilemma is not whether to become rich or not, for it is not the issue. Possessions and money are not the issues here. The test of equality in life is the issue here. It is a question of loyalty to salvation whether a man betrays the principle of equality or not. It is a matter of divine law that has got nothing to do with the abundance of one's possessions. What a man follows at heart is the ordeal in life. The test of spirit is the issue here. What shall it be, dear soul? Equality or inequality? Fairness or power? Reason or madness? Peace or war? Which path do you choose? That is what life is all about! We can give the homeless great fortunes, but it does not guarantee that money will change their lives for the better. Each man makes his own choice in life. It is the faith, not the social status, which determines the path we walk. It is true that in our modern world there are very few rich people that believe in equality. However, it will be foolish of those few altruist rich people to throw away their riches because of the madness of society pertaining inequality. Will a man drown himself because others are drowning? Will a man drown himself because he cannot save others from drowning? Of course not! Equality has got nothing to do with riches or with a social status. Equality is a matter of faith; it is an individual choice, not a political or a social system. Equality is a vision not a division. Therefore, I never condemned rich people because they benefit from the system of inequality. But I condemn all human beings, whether rich or poor, who choose to follow the deadly path of inequality. Because inequality is the epitome of division, and it gives birth to human sufferings. All the exploitations and discriminations which shroud society stem from the jungle law chief principle of inequality. This emanation has also reminded me about the sufferings of many single women in our modern society. The despair of women who wish to get married is equal to the despair of the poor to strike rich. In truth, these patterns are at fallacy. Yes, the dream is not at fallacy, but the deeds are. Deeds that stem from despair only magnify despair and lead one closer to the self destructive vortex of vanity. Particularly in the physical society in which I was both fortunate and unfortunate to live, it happened that I evidenced the despair of single women, whom were, like the deer, standing in line before the lion. On personal account I discovered that my spiritual gift, poetry, helped me to embrace my destiny instead of fretting about it. I found pleasure in poetry, which no money in the world can buy. I believe that if I did not discover my spiritual gift, I would have never evolved spiritually, and never would have, thus, found happiness. Yes, being poor was harsh, and if ever being rich, would be nice for a change, but either way, regardless of my social status and abundance of possessions, I have found my purpose in life owing to poetry. I have found nirvana in my true vocation, not in the world of Man. Therefore the message in this emanation is to abandon the material world and live life by the values of salvation and by carpe diem. We should not be affected by the lies of a rotten world, but follow our inner truth instead. It is true that we cannot always afford to survive in the body, because of the madness occupying human societies, but we can always choose to live life in accordance with salvation. The spiritual world can never be taken away from us. Our inner choice is untouched. When we choose to live life in accordance with the principles of divine law we can never lose life, and we can never miss the goal of free and happy life. Life is about giving and about evolving, not about taking or destroying. Life is about selflessness not about selfishness. Life is about living not about dying. Life is about love, not about fears. Life is about social harmony, not about social disharmony.

Emanation V:     The parable of the city of death


There was once a city called 'The city of death', because human rights
and expressionism were forbidden in it. Moreover, it was not allowed
to feel good in public. Only in secret was a person allowed to rejoice,
but not in society. Thus, anyone who showed signs of joy in public
was hurt and persecuted. Such a person was deemed as an offender of
the social law and tagged as a dangerous person. Any signs of human
interaction could destroy the fragile city of death. One night the
guards of the fortress which protected the city of death drank from the
wine of a nomad. The nomad told the guards that it was the wine of
salvation that he gave them, thus they were very happy to drink it.
Thereupon, they rejoiced, sang, danced, and laughed. The people of
the city of death were asleep at the time, thus the guards left their
posts and went to party with beautiful nomadic women outside the
walls of the city of death. Then the gates were open and all the
primitive invaders from the woods entered through the gates and
destroyed the city of death.

Comments:

This emanation kind of reminded me about the physical reality in Europe. However, I thought about the oppression of human rights as the subject for criticism rather than the external invasion of mass groups. I always believed that it was wrong of people to claim that the destruction of a human society is the devil's fault, or even God's fault. In this metaphor, I believe that if the guards were not oppressed by the rules of their own society, they would have never deserted their posts or even tempted to drink wine during duty, let alone wine rendered to them by a stranger. If a human society oppresses its people to a point of madness, then it is only a matter of time before things go wrong. Moreover, in this parable I thought about angels who follow divine law, and about demons that follow the jungle law. If the guardian angels are tempted by the demons, they might break divine law and doom humanity to destruction. The wine of vanity which made the guards drunk in this parable was offered in the guise of the wine of salvation, which is a liberating wine. However, if it was truly the wine of salvation then the guards would have never been tempted to forsake their posts. They opened the gates for primitive people because they were intoxicated with the wine of vanity, whose side effects are illusions, disorder, apathy, and mindlessness. The paradox of piety within impiety and vice versa, like the paradox of salvation within vanity and vice versa, imply that the city of death is in fact the city of life, and that freedom of human emotions and expressions can lead to the destruction of social order. The collapse of a human society occurs because of either tyranny or anarchy. There is a heavy price that one has to pay in order to live in the city of death, and that price is spiritual life. Hence, one must forfeit salvation in order to survive physical life in vanity, whereas if one only follows salvation, without order, then chaos is looming. See the book 'The balance of justice' for such additional paradoxes.

## Emanation VI:    About divine needs

Dear friends, a man does not always get the chance to pursue his dreams, because the modern world is in a state of chaos. But I tell you the truth, it is better to take the spiritual gifts seriously than to ignore them. Even though we do not get the chance to attain our dreams, we can still embrace the spiritual gift and cherish it. Behold the musician who is desperate to come out with his music. Such a man is perceived as a madman in society. Because of oppression of divine needs such a man looks like as if he has been bitten by a venomous snake. Such a man looks rabid and he even gets frustrated because his evolution was stolen away from him by an ignorant generation. Such a man is not understood by a primitive society, but he is admired by a civilized society. A society which does not give an opportunity to an individual to progress spiritually is basically a backwards society. The needs of a human being are not only physical. Without the satisfaction of divine needs a human being cannot attain happiness. The liberation of a human being begins with evolution through the spiritual gift. The call, the purpose, the mission of the musician is to express oneself through music. If we alienate the musician from society, or suppress his/her needs to evolve spiritually, then we break the social eco system of the divine order. To deprive a musician from music will be equal to eliminate a species from the eco system. Therefore, you better treat the oppressed individual as if he/she was bitten by a snake than to ignore him/her and tag him/her as mad. Because, in fact, an unfulfilled artist is bitten by a snake in the spiritual world when one is oppressed in regard to one's divine needs to evolve. If you ignore a human being who has a dream to evolve with one's spiritual gift, it is similar to ignore that person as if he/she was bitten by a toxic snake in the physical reality. Will you be so cruel to ignore another human being in need of your help? Of course not! Therefore you should be aware of the importance to promote divine needs and help artists in their evolution. A person who aspires to evolve spiritually with one's spiritual gift (or passion) is like a damsel in distress, therefore I urge you to be as kind as chivalrous knights that save the damsel in distress and not as cruel villains that harm her. The social battle of the species in mankind is analogous to a reptile that watched a bird who is trying to fly. The reptile will devour the bird in the first opportunity when the bird is down. Similarly, that what happens to many artists in all world societies when they are mocked, abused, neglected, exploited, oppressed and harmed! The ignorant just claim 'I do not understand the fuss!', when an artist cries out for help to evolve. The cruel and heartless predator is entertained by the sufferings of the sensitive oppressed artist. The brutal predator mocks at the fall of the artist. Friends, it is the seed of salvation, the seed of divine law which makes a man like as if he was bitten by a snake. When a man is writhing on the ground because of emotional distress that is caused by oppression, it is the bite of divine angels, the bite of love that he suffers from. Therefore I urge you, dear friends, to aspire towards social harmony. Please help the individual to discover his/her spiritual gifts, thereupon nurture it. Without the development of art and culture in society, humanity is doomed to remain stuck in the consciousness of the dark ages. Dear friends, the new dawn has arrived. Salvation is at hand. Extend your hands to your fellow man, and help each other to evolve spiritually. Contribute to social harmony by the satisfaction of everyone's divine needs.

Comments:

It should be remarked here that the apathy in human society, which is often accompanied/usurped by mockery against individuals which has a talent, or a dream, or a mission, is the seal of the jungle law. Those who live in the consciousness of vanity are oblivious to life. Thus, they have no pulse and no care in regard to either human or divine needs. Such folks were not born yet in salvation. In that sense their seed of life is dead, and that is why they cannot fathom the need of the individual to express his/her ideas and progress in the spiritual evolution of life. In the reality in which I lived many artists ended in bedlams, jail, hospitals, and graveyards. The fortunate artists found refuge either abroad, or in isolation within society, when they were exempted from the harshness and madness of the rabble, owing to secured economical circumstances. I feel that I have elaborated enough about my personal situation in other books. Thus, it is sufficed to say here that the imbalance in society harms myriads of moralists. The crime of society against the individual begins with the establishment of inequality as a system, and with the creation of social hierarchy in accordance with primitivism. The eradication of the weak in society begins with the collective's nucleus consciousness of power. As for poets, I believe that they are the best of all artists to give account as for the situation in modern society. In a way, poets are like doctors and healers because they are feelers of the earth. Thus, as a poet, I have always felt the urge to correct humanity. For me social harmony meant to disperse vanity and to unite all poets together against war and competition. However, society in my time was not evolved enough to appreciate my efforts to heal humanity. Like many artists I was shunned, ignored, and even oppressed. According to the jungle law; the strong, hence the rich in society was respected and admired, whereas the weak, hence the poor, was disrespected and despised. Thus, the worst that happened to artists was that as soon as they became rich and powerful, they forgot all about the sufferings of other artists. Selfishness, in its monstrous manifestation, usurped moral virtue and reason within such artists and supplied them with madness and love of material comfort. The world has replaced life in their agenda. Tolerance and equality is a matter of evolution, thus I have found it important to impart the knowledge of divine solidarity in order to create awareness of what a human being can become when power over others is invested with one. The progress of society is too slow for the altruist. Thus, I have always felt as if my soul was burning in the inferno of a living hell when I have tried to approach society with my poems, stories, and messages. The biggest problem in modern society is that human rights do not yet exist, and therefore divine rights have no existence. The struggle for the restoration of human rights is therefore crucial in all modern societies, because as soon as human rights are recognized and established, that divine needs and rights will be able to catch root in society. The progress of the individual is vital for the creation of social harmony. If every person got his/her own fair share in society, then there would be peace within society. It should also be noted here that one cannot ignore the fact that there is a damsel in distress in society. The person that chooses to ignore a damsel in distress is an ignorant. However, the person who chooses to harm the damsel in distress and increase her sufferings is no other than a wicked villain. But the person who chooses to help the damsel in distress is a hero. My choice was to promote artists when I had the chance. It was very difficult for other people to understand why I was so dedicated to help and promote others above myself. But I knew the truth that altruism was the antidote for selfishness. I knew that the destruction of our human society was caused by selfishness; therefore I have rebelled against selfishness and promoted other artists before me. I should further mention here that I gave the example of artists in this particular emanation, though not only artists feel hurt by the ignorance of society. In fact, any person with a passion for something, say an astronomer, an anthropologist, a scientist, etc. who has a dream to evolve in accordance with one's passion, is hurt by the oppression of one's divine needs. The madness of society is ignorance and vice versa. Any attempt of an individual to contribute to humanity should be respected by society. When I was the damsel in distress back in the year 2000, Israel was the fool that saw me writhing in the woods. The fool just ignored me, and I simply died of a bite of a toxic snake. When I was a damsel in distress, back in 1997-1999, England was the fool that ignored me and let me die convulsing. Here the fool even kicked me for his amusement while I was dying. When I was the damsel in distress in exile in Denmark, it happened that Denmark was the wicked villain that raped me while I was writhing with deep pain. Here the oppression of my human rights was systematic, brutal, and ruthless. My spiritual gift was exploited, as others have benefited from my labor while I had to sustain poverty and oppression. However, as a damsel in distress that is constantly raped by Danish society I cry out for help that the American nation will save me. The American dream has become my daily supplication. As I groan with pains and bleed to death while I am violated by the savage Danish flock, I fancy the American knight rescuing me. In that sense, the consciousness of the American nation is my liberator. As it happened that many individuals, regardless of their background, have realized their dream owing to the consciousness and progress of the American nation. The fact that my intellectual property received a fair chance in America is giving me hopes that some day I will be liberated from the hell of Denmark.

Emanation VII:     The mirror of truth


Greetings, dear friends. Mirrors never lie, unless they are broken or distorted, thus we should always ascertain that the source of the truth is perfect and that it is as clear as crystal. The critics of society differ in sources, thus the politician and the poet are two different mirrors of society. Friends, the ultimate question of an individual in regard to the social reality is: how can we distinguish between a jungle law society and a divine law society? Some may argue that society is civilized, open, free, and tolerant, whereas others will describe society as the complete opposite. There are two things which we should take into account before we discern or sense the true nature of society. The first thing we should take into account is impartiality. From which source the statements were made? An aggressive tyrant politician or a rich oppressor who thrives on the misery of the people will surely assert that there is nothing wrong in society, whereas the homeless and the poor will testify as for the madness of society. The second thing we should take into account before we judge society is the principle of equality. Is there equality in society? Is there a spirit of brotherhood in society? Is there fairness in society? Those who believe in the principle of equality dismissed their social status and rebelled against the creation of social class. Many of such great rebels are artists. In fact, artists are the emissaries of the light. Owing to the principle of creativity they follow equality. Artists rebel against the jungle law when they create. Any person who follows a meaningful life, with essence and beauty, is the mirror of the truth. Salvation is the polarity of the artists, humanists, altruists, and moralists. Furthermore, the followers of equality live in the real reality of creation, whereas the followers of inequality live in the illusion of power. The realists, the survivalists, and the predatory opportunists all worship the world and follow vanity. Unlike them, the artists, humanists, altruists, and moralists worship life and follow salvation.

Therefore it is known that those who love life and cherish it also follow the principle of Carpe Diem. Power and beauty here are incompatible, because the ugly intentions of a greedy powerful politician (or a business man) cannot be compatible with the pure intentions of a moralist artist. Equality and inequality are two parallel lines. A person can be either partial or impartial but not both. At the same length, a person can either speak the truth or lie, but not both. At the same length, a person can either follow equality or inequality, but not both. Therefore, before we look into the mirror, we should ascertain that we really look into the mirror of the truth. Because the mirror of an honest artist is perfect and clear as a crystal, whereas the mirror of a dishonest rich man is broken and distorted. Hence, the mirror of a dishonest rich man is not the mirror of truth, whereas the mirror of the honest artist is the mirror of truth. Dear friends, in a jungle law society the one who criticizes society is silenced, punished, and abused. Such a critic is depicted as the enemy of society. However, in a divine law society the one whom criticizes society is appreciated, because constructive criticism is like a healer that contributes to social harmony and peace. In fact, any healer in a divine society is rewarded and praised. We should also remember that only in a free open society that a man enjoys the human right to express one's thoughts, art, feelings, and opinions. Freedom of expression in reality is the indicator of society's true nature. In many modern world societies it is not common to look in the mirror of truth. Imagine such intolerant societies as ugly cave women that never cared about their beauty. Such primitive women live in a very low level of evolution that they do not care about their appearance at all. Their external beauty is not important to them. Thus, in the same length, the inner beauty of a human society is not important to the ugly wicked destroyers of society. Therefore, we should take heed before we criticize society. It is like a man waking up in the morning and looking in the mirror. After he washed his face he suddenly discovered a zit on his nose, and noticed that the hair in his nose grew bigger. Such a man can choose whether to beautify his face and make himself presentable and nice before he goes to work or not. When such a man cares about his outlook, he does something positive about it. What makes him civilized is the choice to rebel against his ugliness. Such a man is equated with a civilized society that corrects its wrongs, when an artist (mirror of truth) points it out. If there are vapors in the bathroom that makes the mirror unclear, the civilized man will wash the vapors away from the mirror in order to look more clearly and carefully at his face. Thus, if an artist in society is muffled, unknown, or unexpressed, then the civilized society will help the artist in promotion and appreciate his/her purpose and critics. However, if we will give a mirror to a witch or to a troll, they will smash it, because they cannot tolerate their own ugly sight. Therefore, it is known that in a savage society there is no tolerance towards critics, and that the truth is suppressed. Freedom of expression in general, and freedom of speech in particular, are forbidden in jungle law societies. Imagine artists as mirrors of truth, and here their freedom of expression is violated when the artists are systematically oppressed by the savage society. Dear friends, do not be foolish enough to pose as mirrors of truth before trolls and witches, lest they will smash you to small pieces. If you can sense that your criticism against society will get you into trouble then keep it in secret until evolution will enable the truth to come out. Dear friends, we cannot force beauty and love on society. A society without culture will never appreciate beauty and love, but a cultural society will find you, even when you do not come forward with the truth. Remember, it is a choice of a man to wash away the vapors from his mirror. Thus, if society wishes to evolve in beauty and grace, then society will find you, call you, cherish you, and promote you. Surely we should never give up our struggle to promote the truth in society. Surely we should never give up the principle of creativity. The truth is a liberator, but not all societies are ready to be liberated, and therefore we might get hurt in our attempt to transform society. Dear friends, we cannot impose aestheticism, progress, and culture on society, but we can hope that our efforts to beauty and purify society will some day be appreciated. However, if society is a divine law society then go ahead and speak up your mind and promote the truth.

Comments:

My knowledge in this emanation is empirical, though I must admit
that like many other moralists and artists, I have tried to impose
progress, beauty, and culture on modern world societies; a fact that
only caused me grief and misery. Retrospectively, it feels as if I was
posing as a mirror of truth in front of ugly witches, before I was
smashed to small pieces time after time. At one point I have realized
that progress cannot be imposed and that I could only get more hurt
by society because of my efforts to liberate the weak and oppressed.
The clashes between my messages of love and society's attempt to
impose conformism to the jungle law on me resulted in a stalemate. I
refused to give in to society's Madness, whereas society refused to
accept my Reason (moral virtue, etc.) At last I have settled with the
conclusion that progress cannot be imposed on society and therefore I
continued to create in secret. Before my mysterious epic journey in
exile has commenced I dwelled on the illusion that freedom of speech
was fundamental in all world societies. My naïve upbringing and
altruistic approach stemmed from equality. But with such a naive
stance I have found myself in troubles endless of times, never to really
fathom that the world of man was not what I thought it was. The
literature lessons in high school deceived me. Thus, I have felt rage
against my literature teachers, as I have learned how ignorant and
misleading they were in regard to the truth of what the world is. My
realism brought me gradually to a point of madness, despair, and
solitude. Human society despised the truth of its function. The jungle
law was supreme and no follower of the jungle would break the jungle
law in order to allow love, peace, and freedom to grow. As an altruist I
have realized that the real terrorists were in fact the elitists of modern
societies. The leaders of jungle law societies promoted fear, worries,
and terror in order to establish the rule of the jungle law super
organism. Because of the massive incitement and brainwash of the

rabble by the incorporated media, I was not even allowed to mention the fact that I was from Israel, let alone to speak about individual love. My journey in exile was one big long inferno, like an agonizing death of a soul. Then I looked around and noticed that there were many other individuals, just like me, whom were oppressed beyond belief. If I did not take the plunge and walked the walk, I might have dismissed the monstrosity of Danish society, and settled on the terms 'far fetched' and 'Science fiction reality'. But because I was so deeply hurt with depressions and because of my impact with a savage society that I have found my potential as a liberator. Generally speaking, all artists are liberators, because of their progress in evolution. Thus, I felt sorry for other artists and humanists, because I have went through the same nightmarish ordeal. I dreamt about saving our planet earth. I dreamt about saving other artists, but first I had to save myself, and here I was constantly at loss. In Denmark there was no difference between a terrorist and a critic. In the eyes of Danish society any critic of society was a potential terrorist. As a humanist I have criticized China, Denmark, Israel, England, and even Sweden, but always from an individual point of view, and always out of personal experience. Unlike the incorporated media which serve the jungle law super organism, I have spoken the truth out of a human experience. The individual is the mirror of truth not the incorporated media. In every society I have found the nationalists as the thugs of the jungle law. But those who followed justice are like fellow doves of salvation. In my experience the incorporated media in Denmark was probably the most vicious and cruel tool of the jungle law super organism. Denmark probably was not the biggest evil in the world. However, Denmark was probably the most sophisticated evil in the world as it managed to conceal its atrocious crimes against humanity in very a manipulative way. There were two fronts in which the presiding evil managed to deceive everyone. The first front was through intensive internal oppression of human beings. Here through the rule of fear and through mass brainwash and harassments, a human being was muffled and euthanized until no one dared to speak the truth against Danish society. The second front, in which, I assume, the shield of Denmark was situated, was the public relations propaganda. Here Danish society recruited endless of liars to praise Denmark abroad. The surveys which the incorporated media spread were based on one big deception, that Denmark was a garden of roses. An impartial spectator that never plunged into the depth of Danish realism might swallow the lie and believe that Denmark was a saint nation. But as an individual who lived in Denmark, under the oppression of Danish society, like many other afflicted individuals I was enraged by the sophisticated manipulation of the elitists. The stealthy hierarchy, the social classes, the madness of socialism, the systematic oppressions of all classes, and the ruling negative spirit of war were hidden from the world public because the world public have already been brainwashed to think that Denmark was a heaven on earth. The sad thing was, in my view, the fact that many artists in Denmark were bought by the jungle law super organism, and by thus, they have betrayed the truth. Instead of speaking up against oppression, they have joined it. Thus, the truth was always kept secret, whereas the lie was spread world wide. A human being in Denmark was left without human rights and without the opportunity to progress in life, whereas the animalist joined the collective oppression because of material rewards such as comfort, money, and power. Thus, world opinion was already forged on the collective lie which was dictated and chanted, by the myriads of followers of the Jante/Jungle law alliance, both in Denmark and aboard. The victory of the jungle law was achieved by the rule of inequality in Denmark and by the success of the incorporated media to supply Denmark with a good image. Sadly, the testimonies of thousands of individuals who suffered in Denmark, including mine, were muffled and overruled because of the manipulation of world opinion. The solidarity of the jungle law super organism is a reality based on ignorance, greed, material comfort, apathy, and most of all on vanity. The ordinary tourist that takes a photo of the statue of the little mermaid cannot hear the cries of help of a raped foreign woman in a brothel nearby because her voice is muffled. The same goes with the cries of refugees, as their evidence have been marginalized by the promotion of a vain culture. Drinking from foul sewage of the incorporated media means spiritual death. Thus, the rabble's consciousness has been made dumb and beastly. I should mention here, in regard to freedom in a society that freedom has got nothing to do with a political system in theory, but only in practice. It happens in many so called democratic societies that people get into trouble with the authorities because they speak the truth against the wrongs of their societies. It means that what an individual experience in reality is the true nature of society and not what a political system may suggest. I have experienced the oppression of the artist myself for many years and on many occasions. My solidarity with the weak and with the oppressed in society put me in the front line against the jungle law. However, I knew that the core of divine law was solidarity with the weak and the liberation of the oppressed. I knew that equality is the way to salvation, and therefore I adhered to my mission to combat inequality, not only in Denmark, but in all world societies. The way I criticized China and other world societies, was through literature and art. However, I did it because of my solidarity with the weak in China. A Tibetan or a Chinese under classed would face big troubles had they wrote the books I have written about China and Tibet. Thus, I was hoping that someone in America would take my case against Denmark and tell the public the truth about the oppression of human rights in this society. When I think about this book in general I feel like a lecturer from the future. I do not think that I could withstand the task of giving a lecture in front of an audience because of my stress level. However, I feel as if I am standing in front of an audience from either the past or the future. The corridors of time, in which I walked, led me to a very strange auditorium. As for always being skeptic about the true nature of society, I spoke from a point of view in which I was advocating for the weak in society. There was no amount of money that could dissuade me from seeking justice, fairness, and equality in society. I did not live the war of the social class, but resided in the serenity that came from peace and equality. The love of life was the source of my perspective, not the vanities of the world, for life is beautiful not the world. The world of mankind, the system of Man, is just an illusion, or rather choreography. We did not come to the world to settle down and rot on its illusions and vanities, we have come to evolve and progress in spiritual life.

Emanation VIII:     A man's worth


Dear friends, the way society values a human being should be challenged since many individuals went astray because of the distortion of the truth. Friends, there are two systems by which a man is judged, the first system is the jungle law and the second system is divine law. You may wonder 'is there anything in between those two systems?' so let me retort with the following question, 'When a man is put on trial can the jury choose to be neutral?' Have no doubt about it: no one can remain impartial when it gets to motion, hence when it comes to judgment. Consciousness imposes an absolute law, hence, when we deem and judge a human being in society we cannot remain impartial. However, we can choose to follow good motives without undermining the principles of fairness and equality. It means that our faith determines our way of judgment. Prejudice stands against fairness each time we engage in any social interaction. Often we hear the instruction 'Do not judge others' as it meant against the negative sense. A man can choose whether he is an advocate or a prosecutor of other human beings as a matter of principle. The advocate, with his compassionate stance will judge in accordance with fairness and equality, whereas the prosecutor, with his vindictive stance, will judge in accordance with power and inequality. The advocate of human beings is an ethicist that follows divine law by faith, whereas the prosecutor of human beings is a predator that follows the jungle law by faith. Dear friends, before we judge a human being we already establish a general approach, therefore I urge you always to follow divine law and always to have the approach of the advocate. Do not ever judge by bias, prejudice, or bigotry, because if you do not give others the benefit of the doubt you are depriving yourselves from salvation. If you do not approach your fellow human beings with compassion and understanding, then you divest yourselves from grace, honor, and light. Before we get the facts about any human being we should adapt to divine law within our hearts. When we give other human beings a chance to show their good side, we redeem ourselves from the constrictions of predatory judgment. Then there are the facts of the truth that can help you to judge more clearly despite your divine approach. It means that when you are cheated or robbed by a man whom you trusted, even your compassionate approach cannot change the fact that you have been hurt by such a man. However, the conclusion not to trust the man who cheated you should not impair your judgment in regard to others. Not all human beings can be trusted; but if you change your approach from divine law to jungle law, you only increase your pain. There is no reward in prejudice, only worries and concerns. But if you learn the lesson not to trust others despite your good intentions, you win both in approach and in pragmatism. First I wish to advise you here not to judge others unless you have no choice. It means that when you pass judgment on someone who did not interact with you in reality you are getting involved with gossip. Be careful not to be hasty to judge, because the super flock mentality of modern world society is often pressing you to judge others. Stay away from gossip and remain loyal to the principles of fairness and equality. This way you will remain pure at heart and peaceful at mind. Be careful not to be poisoned by society's mass brainwash to judge people in accordance with social status, power, money, fame, etc. Every human being on earth has a big value, so do not waste your value by devaluing others because of prejudice. It is wise to be cautious in all engagements with other human beings, particularly in predatory societies, but do not allow anything or anyone to pollute your hearts or your minds in regard to valuing other human beings. The worth of a human being is often hidden, but I tell you the truth, a man's worth is measured by a man's merits, not by his money and/or possessions. In jungle law societies human beings are valued by the standards of society, and not by the truth of what they really worth. But according to divine law a man's worth is measured by a man's deeds, merits, virtues, and faith. The following parable may illumine the importance of one's worth: Once there was a business man who had two sons, one was his own son and the other was his step son. This man always favored his own son over his step son, thus, he always valued his own son more than his step son. But one day they went on a family trip in nature and the father fell into a wild river. The man's wife and his real son could not swim, thus he felt lost when he asked for their help from the water. However, the step son was a great swimmer and a courageous athlete. At once the step son plunged into the wild river and saved his step father from drowning. From that day on the rich businessman valued both his two sons equally. Therefore I urge you to judge by merits and by good motives, and not by possessions, and not by genetic inheritance or anything else that is associated with vain pride. The worth of a human being should be measured by deeds, faith, and merits. Be humble before you judge others, and be compassionate in your judgment, but do not let the facts of the truth subvert you even when you have been cheated by others. Watch out that you do not follow the mainstream of society that praises the rich and condemns the poor. Always follow fairness and equality before you judge others. A man's true worth has got nothing to do with material comfort, money, social class, or vain pride.

Comments:

There is more to this subject, in fact more than I could have possibly elaborated upon in one letter. There is the issue of war heroes which is another distortion, for how can anyone who murdered other human beings be accepted by society as a hero. It is against divine law to kill other human beings; however society made an exception to such a crime because of either pragmatism or nationalism. But in either case, society promotes a criminal as a matter of fact. Society can justify war by the need to survive; it means that a war hero in such a case is deemed by society as a liberator, even though he killed many other human beings. Nevertheless, such a man is still a criminal in the courts of divine law, because survival is the manifestation and agenda of the jungle law. Whether society is a survivalist in a case of self defense, or just a realist in a case of petty dispute, the war hero is still valued by society as a high class citizen by the vice of murder. It is even worse when a nation is a predatory opportunist, like in the case of imperialism, when the war hero killed many other human beings for the sake of avarice. In all three cases a war hero is valued by the expectations and conventions of a jungle law society. The fact that the crime is collective does not mitigate the crime of the war hero soldier. Unlike the super flock choice to send individuals to either kill or die, we should examine the motives of athletes and artists before we can determine their true worth. Nationalists cannot be equally worth to individualists. The individualist, unlike the nationalist is serving divine law. The truth of evolutionary progress is first and foremost individual. As an author I never represented Israel, and if any person wishes to give credits to the nation of Israel because of my achievements, he or she is, in my experience, a heartless idiot. All these years of my hard labor in exile had nothing to do with nationalism. I was faithful to the consciousness of salvation, not bound by the ignorance of nationalism. I served humanity not my nationality. In fact, Israel only hurt me, when it betrayed me, and I have denounced its adherence to the jungle law. I remained loyal to divine law by pursuing my spiritual gift of poetry. The individual's quest is the service that completes others and contributes to harmony and peace. There is no higher purpose for a human being than to serve the divine order. Hence, when a man has to choose between his own country and his own spiritual gift (true vocation) it is his choice that determines his true worth. A fool will run to the gun and wave with the flag; such a fool is a dogmatic jungle law worshipper. However, a knight will run to the gallery and paint from the bottom of his heart; such a knight is an altruist devotee of divine law. Often it is the altruist who is accused by the nationalist for being selfish, but the truth is the complete opposite, for those who choose to follow nationalism are selfish in their core, whereas those who choose to follow their divine contract are the harmonists of humankind. Therefore, it is by a choice that we determine our true worth in life. The way the world judge a human being is equal to the perspective of demons, whereas the way life judges a human being is equal to the perspective of angels. Nevertheless, the social eco system accepts all species without discrimination. Thus, both predators and prey have an equal value from the perspective of the earth. In the book 'The balance of justice' I have elaborated upon the two inhuman laws that in fact influence our worth and value. On many personal an account I have been subjected to abuse, neglect, harassment, intimidations, discriminations, exploitations, and cheating in Denmark, a fact which made me stronger in my rebellion against the jungle law super organism. The individual despises the rulers in power in Denmark because of the abuse to which one is subjected on a daily basis. Thus, I have learned not to trust everyone blindly because of my bitter experiences. Furthermore, my skepticism sense has been enhanced due to an evolutionary need. My approach is still divine, and I still advocate for all human beings. But when I discover the truth about the true nature of a person I allow myself to judge in accordance with fairness and equality. I believe, however, that in all modern world societies the jungle law rules in power. In Denmark the way a human being was judged was the epitome of the jungle law. The construction of the social class was a typical jungle law erection. Here a human being was judged, tagged, and treated in accordance with dogmatic mundane criteria such as nationality, race, religion, culture, background, riches, possessions, occupation, and other such vanities. The lower class is poked like a wounded animal in a zoo's cage, until one is driven to madness or crime. The system of the jungle law, vanity, was beyond description. However, despite the horrible experiences with many people in Denmark, the jungle law organism failed to poison me to hate everybody else, or to think that everyone else are my enemy. I have met many righteous, decent, and honest Danish individuals who resented the social system in Denmark just as much as foreigners did. However, such horrible and traumatic experiences for so many years made me extremely recluse and lonely in Denmark. The atrocious antagonism of the individual in Danish society had an impact upon me, thus I have imploded with depressions and found refuge in my poetry. Thus, my spiritual gift was my redeemer. Sadly the creation of a diabolical social hierarchy in Denmark made it impossible for dozens of thousands of individuals to evolve spiritually. The worst part here was that the strong in this jungle law society gets the right to crush the weak. Such madness, which in any other society would require reprimand, here is met with promotion and praise. There was no respect between human beings, but only valuation in accordance with social status. The lotto winner was a hero, but the unemployed is always the zero; thus the lotto winner was worshipped and praised while the unemployed was oppressed and cursed. The rabble was consisted of wild animals that worshipped inequality. It is my hope that in the future the jungle law will be toppled down and replaced by divine law.

He who judges by vanity,

Money, power, and possessions;

Has drifted away from sanity,

Like the death of many nations.


But he who judges by salvation,

Merits, fairness, and equality;

Is blessed with the pure elation,

That saves humanity.

## Emanation IX:    A mind of your own

Dear friends, greetings. When we study the stars above we learn that some of them spin and some of them do not spin. In some stars there is motion whereas in others there is no motion. But all the stars have one thing in common; they are all affected by the magnetic field of the universe. It means that since the universe is in constant motion even the non dynamic stellar objects are in fact in a constant motion. However, stellar motion here is equated with free will and with social interaction in regard to human beings, as some human beings have a mind of their own, whereas others choose to follow the drift of society obediently and without any mind of their own. In that sense all stars that have motion in them are in fact rebels, and here we know as a fact that a star without motion is a star without life. Hence, life on other planets is bound by motion. Our blue planet is a planet with a mind of its own, as it spins and revolves around like a dancer in the universe. When the earth will stop spinning it will be the end of our civilization and the end of all forms of life on earth, as the magic of the earth is also depended on the affects of the sun and the moon upon it. That is why I urge you, dear friends, to always question the drifts of the mainstream in society. Skepticism and wonderment are redeemers, because the drift of modern society is the drift of self destruction. It is not a secret that our earth is on the verge of destruction, but we can still save it and we can still heal it before it is too late. The importance of freedom of consciousness is vital as for the restoration of the social eco system balance. If the drift of society is to go to war, then a scientist can rebel against it and not join the war. The jungle law is like a black hole that destroys all small planets and stars, therefore those who rebel against it will be safe, even on the account of the loss of the physical body. The scientist that was faced with the dilemma whether to join the war that the masses dictated, or to follow his own peaceful gift had a very tough time in making up his mind. On one hand he was faced with charges of treason if he declined the offer to serve his predatory jingoistic country, but if he agreed to join the war, on the other hand, then he would be equated with a dead star. Friends, don't ever give up your motion, lest you'd be devoured by the vortex of spiritual death. Vanity has many storms in life but we can always win when we choose to remain loyal to motion (salvation). The scientist, if failed to flee his war monger country, had to choose between life and death of his spirit. But I tell you the truth, every individual, in all world societies have to go through the same dilemma of whether to join the drift of the jungle law or to remain faithful to divine law. The madness of the rabble is the furnace of corruption. The crusade to follow riches of money and to attain power of social status is the road to self destruction. However, an individual can break free from the massive stressful tides of society owing to the choice to follow one's own spiritual gift. Therefore I urge you, dear friends, to restore freedom of consciousness in all world societies, and have a mind of your own. Do not let society dictate you what is right and what is wrong. The way to a happy life is through personal evolution not through collective demolition. Pertaining literary criticism we can posit the analogy of flat dogmatic characters in a story to hollow people in real life that follow society blindly and without question, but a round character, whether a hero or a villain, is always dynamic. In that analogy a dynamic human being is like either a black hole (villain) or like a nebula (hero). The non dynamic human being, hence, the flat character, is in fact a boring dead star. Therefore, I must warn you, dear friends, that having a mind of one's own can also be a dangerous thing when it turns negative, but it is still better than not having a mind of one's own at all. Because the villain can always become a hero at one point of revolution and vice versa, but a flat character has no chance for salvation unless it becomes dynamic. Dear friends, we have all born to this world as individuals, and yes, for the common good, it is important that we interact as equal human beings. In fact, we complete each other and cannot live outside of society because of our fragile needs, but when the super flock mentality is off balance we must be aware of its madness and dissociate ourselves from the madness of society. When society is ruled by reason it is the liberator of the individual. However, when society is ruled by madness, the individual is the liberator of society owing to one's reason, moral virtue, and spiritual gift. In the balance between the individual and the collective there shouldn't be neither authority nor power of one body over the other, but the collective and the individual should interact equally and share rights equally in order to attain social harmony. Therefore, we should always protest against violations of human rights in all world societies, and struggle to restore human rights in all world societies. Having a mind of one's own can be devastating to society when one follows the jungle law, but when one follows divine law having a mind of one's own can be liberating. Dear friends, pay heed, the danger of automatism is fatal, because all automatons are connected to the mainframe of the jungle law super organism. Thus, the self destruction of a human being occurs already in conformism to a society that worship material comfort and money and abide by the primitive jungle law. Therefore, dear friends, I beseech you to save yourselves from the madness of social automatism and to rebel against all jungle law societies. Remain faithful to divine law and to your true call/vocation in life. When you have a mind of your own, and when you follow your true call/vocation in life you can never lose, for salvation always triumph over vanity, despite of the consequences in the physical reality. Do not let any flock mentality impair your judgment, for love is the emissary of the truth, and the truth is the way to salvation. Be true to yourself and serve only the divine order. Be individuals, think individually, because there are many species of fish in the sea, but if you choose to follow the destructive super flock mentality of the rabble then rest assured that in the end you will be just another shark in a sea of sharks that eat each other. Such a sea of blood is doomed to die out of life because of the broken balance of the eco system. At the same time I ask you to respect other individuals in society and to promote the weak in society. We can only enjoy the harvest of social harmony when we preserve the social balance of equality. All individuals have a place in society without discrimination and without harassments. All individuals on earth were born for a divine reason. When an individual chooses to forfeit one's mind and heart for the sake of the collective, then one loses one's true essence and identity until one becomes a flat character without a meaning and without a reason. Vanity recruited millions of individuals to join its polarity through the rule of inequality. Riches, selfishness, pride, and power are the loots of the hunter, but morals, altruism, modesty, and beauty are the rewards of the shepherd. Friends, rebel against material comfort and return to the haven of your individualism, for evolution without motion is an impossibility.

Comments:

The diffusion that accompanied me all of my life, in recent years made me wish for helpers in order to deliver the messages in a more organized way. Confusion, unlike diffusion, only followed me in regard to the interaction with society, as my adherence to divine law only pushed me more and more out of society, because society was chiefly predatory. I sought refuge many times, but realized that such a request has become a luxury. The physical reality was my hell because of my failure to join the masses in their crusade to destroy life and worship vanity. My rebellion against vanity in the physical world caused me endless of miseries and I often found myself on the verge of dissolution. However, despite of the circumstances outside, it happened that inside me I have found an inner peace. It was a deep serenity that often irked many jungle law automatons in society. The fact that I have had a mind of my own, and found peace of my own attracted many abusers. Impact with society was devastating for me, thus, I have lived recluse in order to preserve both my sanity and my chastity. Because I have been so detrimentally affected, or rather ill treated by society that I find this message extremely important; I feel deeply sorry for so many people who couldn't say no to an evil society when they were brainwashed to go to war or to toil for vanity. On my personal accounts, the worst for me was in England, as here I have been subjected to daily abuse because I was not an automaton. However, the realization of the true construction of the jungle law at that time made me realize that the jungle law existed, and sadly now ruled, also my homeland, and even in Denmark, in which it was sophisticatedly concealed. The 'We and you' systematic propaganda led me to the inference that equality was marginalized whereas power (inequality) was cardinalized. 'If you are not with us, then you are against us' is something that I have heard before as a child, but not in the same intensity as it was in England, and subsequently in Denmark.

The solidarity of the wolf and its pack order was feeding on the mind-control of all individuals. The assimilation of all minds created a super master mind consciousness which is equal to a magnetic field by a black hole. To my horror I have discovered that there is no right to be an individual whom is not part of the collective consciousness. A person with the slightest difference from the mainstream was harassed because of the rule of intolerance. The elimination of freedom of consciousness, and the elimination of the right of privacy in Denmark made the order of the pack convenient for the elitists. Riches and material comfort were promoted even through television programs for children. Retrospectively thinking, I wish that I was an eagle in the beginning of my journey in exile, for then I would have survived reality without depressions. However, because I have been a dove of peace it happened that I have been consumed by Danish society. For me the novel realization that the mind of a human being is so feeble and easy to tamper with only came when it happened to me. Many times I asked my self, 'Why? Why are people so fanatic about their ideology? Why can't they just enjoy life and appreciate the songs of the birds in the mornings?' Only in recent years, however, it has occurred to me that many people are lost, and that their mind had no real foundation. My mind was affected by it as well, but at the end of the day I have always returned to the truth of Carpe Diem. Life is beautiful, life is a gift; life is a precious treasure. Thus, in as much as I have tried to save myself I discovered that by helping others I have in fact also helped myself to overcome brainwash. The ruling spirit of a modern society is bound by the jungle law. The economy in Denmark forced the weak to work and serve the strong. After I broke free from my modern slavery I recall that I was asked to take an education in order to take care of handicap people. 'Shall a handicap take care of another handicap?' I asked the social worker in protest as she chose to ignore the truth about my own file. But in Denmark the exceptions are given often to the swindlers, whereas the righteous and honest are oppressed. In Denmark it was the economy, in Israel it was the army, in England it was the social class. Thus, I only snapped out of the mass brainwash after I cracked down mentally with excruciating pain. As for being a dynamic person in mind, I should add here that the Yin and the Yang interaction and counteraction is much better than the Sha (stagnation) in society, because the Sha person is a flat character that can be forged to join the negative drift without realizing it. Hence, people without character and without any real opinion can be very dangerous when they are used by negative leaders. The known dictum 'Don't ask what your country can do for you, but what you can do for your country' is a horrible lie. The truth is the dictum 'Don't ask what humanity can do for you, but what you can do for humanity'. Humanity is the reason that we are born with spiritual gifts, divine calls, divine missions, divine contracts, true vocations, and divine reasons, not a country. Humanity triumphs over nationalism. I feel sorry for all the poor souls who were dressed with uniforms and supplied with weapons in order to die for a national flag. There has been a distortion of the truth and a use of propaganda by the jungle law drift to go to war. Here the individual was required to forfeit and sacrifice the precious purpose of his life in order to serve the jungle law. The manipulation of the mind in Denmark was very cruel, as here many individuals have fallen victim before the jungle law. Danish society was an underworld society, like a burrow of snakes that slithered and conspired, the silence of the Danes was in fact a prowl for an opportunity to devour the free minded individual. The consciousness of the jungle law group is often using manipulation in order to subdue the individual victim. If you are a sparrow the collective will tell you that you are an eagle, and that you have come to hunt them down and devour them. However, in reality the jungle law collective will consume you because you have wings, and because you follow the law of salvation. Thus, when guilt is inserted in the mind of the sparrow like poison, it takes a very short time before the sparrow is subdued, and subsequently consumed by the snakes. Moreover, it is typical for dogmatic societies to systemize everything by the distortion of the truth and by the infusions of fear and guilt. In robotic jungle law societies if you have a mind of your own, or if you are on the verge of autism, or if you have a stroke of a genius, you'd be tagged as the enemy of society, and subsequently be targeted. It means also that if you are disconnected somehow from the collective consciousness of the group you pose a threat and a danger for the group. Therefore, I thought that this particular message was a key message that can determine a reality of either peace or war. The divine revolution can only win when all individuals advocate for peace out of free will. The collective is not always right, but the divine call of the individual is never wrong.

## Emanation X:     Beastly grace vs. Divine grace

Greetings, friends, peace and love upon you. We, the doves, know the truth of our existence on earth; we live the truth, and envision the truth. Moreover, the truth is the source of our inner peace and happiness. We perceive life as a precious gift; hence, we appreciate the gift of life every day. We love nature and we care for the earth. The truth, our faith, is that we are only visitors in this world. Nevertheless, we are visitors with a divine purpose, which is to evolve in the spirit. It feels great to serve others. It feels great to contribute to social harmony and toil for the healing of the earth. Friends, we are loyal to the law of angels which is the highest law. It is the law of love and peace, fairness and equality, moral virtue and reason, care and sensibility. But friends, often we are told that this world, the earth, is not our world. Often we are told that this world belongs to the wolves only, and that it is by the grace of the beast that we are allowed to become the slaves of the jungle law followers. Dear friends, we should dismiss such lies, for it is by the grace of the divine order that the beast exists. Everything in the world, every creature, whether a prey or a predator, was created by the grace of the divine order, hence, we should not pay attention to reptilian nonsense that is emitted by the jungle law followers. Dear friends, paradoxically as it may sound it is a declaration of truth: survival is not the goal. Yes, we survive physical life as a matter of need and necessity, and we even survive as a matter of want, but we should never worship survival or anything else which stems from vanity and the jungle law. Physical realism is illusive, deceptive, and counteractive, for the real life is in the spiritual realm. Friends, the global money system, which was first created as a need for social balance in regard to credits and rights have been abused by the spirit of the age. Often you hear about rich corrupt people giving money to the needy and bragging that without the grace of the beast the poor would not have survived. But I tell you the truth, without the poor, the rich would never survive the spiritual realm, unless they break the jungle law and comply with divine law. Hence, a humble pure rich man will not claim that his donations were in accordance with the grace of the beast, but he will be delighted to serve the principle of equality without vain pride. Therefore, when you help others, do not ever take pride in your help and claim that it was in accordance with the ego, for the grace of the beast is a product of the jungle law. When you help the weak and needy, you should be happy about it, but do not give credits to yourself. Give credits for the weak and needy, because they promote you in divine deeds, and it is owing to them that you are purified and become a better person. Be humble and modest and serve equality, dear doves. Dear friends; the money system is not based on the law of the beast in theory, but in practice it is based on inequality, exploitations, competitions, power, war, and on the promotion of the self. The money system is serving the wolves to the full, because the law and spirit of mankind are based on vanity by a collective choice. Dear friends, the wolves claim that it is by the grace of the beast that we survive, or are even allowed to survive, but this is not the truth. In fact, it is quite the opposite, for the meek will inherit the earth. It is the selfless, the humble, who is the real inheritor of salvation. It is by free will that a man decides whether to serve war or peace. Stay faithful to divine law and rebel against the jungle law, dear friends. Be careful not to join the jungle law here, for the world belongs to everyone equally. Do not break the balance of equality because of your free will, or because you are tempted by the super flock mentality to become rich in money and possessions. Real wealth dwells in service of others humbly. The real treasure is in fulfilling the divine contract. The real gold is the spiritual gift. Rebel against material comfort, for it is vanity. Remain obedient to salvation, serve creation and promote evolution. It is by the grace of the divine that all things exist. Friends, this world belongs to everyone, so do not ever discriminate anyone. Those who discriminate others are criminals in the courts of divine law. Anyone who breaks the principle of equality is an offender of divine law. All those who discriminate others, in fact cut themselves off from the tree of salvation. Thereupon, they rot on the ground and become food for rats. You, dear doves, should stay growing happy on the tree of salvation, and shine with majesty, grace, and beauty. Do not ever discriminate other human beings. Do not look down at other people, or value them as less. Do not antagonize your fellow man. We are all children of the great universe, free, fair, and equal. We are all part of the earth. Unite, dear doves, heal, and amend, and do not ever break the balance of divine harmony. Whatever you do to others comes back at you like a boomerang; it is the law of the universe. What goes around comes around and vice versa. We must abide by divine law.

Comments:

As a child it is more traumatic to hear jungle law followers
discharging at others, and/or reciting the jungle law. But the worst
that a child can experience is to be subjected to such a malicious
propaganda. Not to be welcomed somewhere because one is different
or because one adheres to divine law, or to be banished from society
because one's parents are from another country, is a sad
contemporary reality. As a parent I am extremely devastated and hurt
by the separation of children from their parents because of
immigration laws. Denmark, just like Israel, became an inhuman
society as both nations broke divine by expelling the parents of
children to their homelands, leaving the children with the horrible
dilemma to choose between their parents and their homeland.
However, the discrimination takes place both by the law of man,
which is stipulated and announced, but also by the jungle law, which
is hidden in society. In my personal experience, as I am often
engrossed with bitter memories pertaining the pain of being
discriminated, my poetry in Israel was rejected on grounds of racism.
The question 'Your mother is from morocco?', which I was so often
asked with a tinge of rage, made it clear to me that the social class in
modern Israel was created by the jungle law followers. When I was
told that my poetry was rejected because of my mother's background,
I tried to explain that my mother had immigrated to Israel as a young
child, and that she hardly knew her birth land. It means that I did not
have any roots in Morocco at all, also because I grew up in orphanages
and Kibbutzim. I was neither ashamed nor proud of my mother's
background; I was simply stating the facts, when I was asked about it.
However, it struck me badly that it meant so much for the publishers
and for the general mass in Israel. I could understand that in England
my poetry was rejected because I was not an Englishman, although I
believe that one should be judged only by merits, but to be rejected in

my own homeland because of my mother's background is outrageous. In Denmark my poetry was rejected because I was tagged as an anomaly. The fact that I did not belong to any specific group sufficed to discriminate me as an individual. The additional discriminations on grounds of racism and nationalism only added to my dismay, and decreased my chances to be accepted in society as a poet. The rage of the mainstream in each country was based on the jungle law and on the dogmas of the grace of the beast. I knocked on the doors of society in good faith and with good intentions, but the doors were smacked in my face because of the rule of intolerance that governed society. The accusation of 'Are you an emigrant?' to which I was subjected in Israel during visits, was equally malicious as the accusation of 'Are you an immigrant?' to which I was subjected in England and in Denmark for so many years in exile. I should note here, however, that in England my service was of a two years contract only. Moreover, the social status madness was also very politically oriented in exile, and had I was not aware of the demonic incitement of the incorporated media, I would have surely testified that the European rabble have swallowed wild cats each time they barged at me 'Are you from Israel?'. Gradually I grew weary of the ignorance of the general mass, and thus resorted to recluse. I have found pastures in my poetry and reminisced. However, the war is between light and darkness, thus, I have found refuge in the inner light despite the external darkness of exile. However, I was mourning many people who had fallen victims to the darkness of society and therefore I have accepted my role as a redeemer. In my heart I deeply wanted to save the people of my age, but they were about to take me with them down to the vortex of hell. Therefore, I have made a leap in time, and wrote the messages from the eye of the hurricane. We need to be careful, because when society is ruled by the jungle law, it only leads to destruction. I advised other good hearted individuals in Denmark to proclaim the defense against the madness of the savage concept of a beastly grace. 'This is our country, and if you do not like it here then you can just go back to your own country' has become the biblical hackney punch lines of the jingoistic bigot. The absurdity of the pathetic savage can also be tackled through humor, but I have learned that there are also other ways to avoid hearing it. Nevertheless, appeasing the beast is quite effective, as here there is a chance for progress and a possible future transformation. It can be done through music, art, and literature. When I wrote 'The adventures of Catrine and the devil II' I felt that I was helping the weak in Denmark. Because the jungle law followers are the weak in the spiritual realm. One can choose to chase a stray dog away with stones and sticks, or to give it a medical care and try to save it. It means one can choose between harshness and kindness in this matter. The choice is rather between hatred and compassion. In my experience, I have made the wrong decision, although I would have never chosen the way of the sword. For me, the choice, according to my belief, was either to ignore the madness of the wicked or to help the wicked to transform and become good. Sadly, I have made the wrong decision, not in theory, but in practice, for the stray dog was infected with rabies. I was bitten by it and now I suffer from incurable depressions. I took a big hit by trying to help Danish society to evolve. Trying to make contact with the Danish physical reality was a fatal mistake, but that is the option between the devil and the deep blue sea. No man can live in solitude forever, and loneliness took the worst affect on me, until madness was about to consume me. However, in all modern societies the hunters say the same things to the doves, but in all societies in which I visited I told the hunters that we, the doves, are on service, and that I was a volunteer on earth. The hunters did not understand what I was talking about because they lived in the darkness and bigotry of the physical world. Their preoccupation with the jungle law and their predominance have clouded their judgment altogether. This message, upon which I also elaborated in other notes, writings, and books, is vital because there is a danger to be brainwashed by the jungle law biggest fallacy that human beings own the earth.

Emanation XI:     The real businessman


Dear friends, the prestige of being a successful businessman is naturally appealing to many people. However, after a considerable effort to understand the individual's true essence, it is the truth that such a dream could be, in fact, the way to vanity. When we look at the bees, or at the ants, they have a social order that is similar to ours, only that their queen is not corrupt, but natural and chaste. In the order of man, it is often the reptilian, the predator, hence the selfish and destructive Alpha leader person that sits in power of riches and authority. It is not a question of being a realist, but rather a test of being a moralist, that a man should ask himself, is it really what I was born to do on earth? Was I born to rule in vanity? Or was I born to do something grand and divine? Many rich businessmen abide by the jungle law rules of power and opportune, but deep inside them there is another businessman. The real businessman inside them is hidden in their spiritual gift and spiritual call. But because of the material world, and because they follow material comfort and money, that they fail to discover their true vocation and true self. Love is wasted when one follows the bigotry and dogmas of the jungle law. Money, comfort, and power are not the goal. The goal is an individual contract that serves social harmony, peace, freedom, love, and salvation. The attachment to the physical reality is the cause for a man's dissociation from his divine seed. Dear friends, we are all businessmen on earth by divine contracts. The successful businessman is the person whom cherishes life and abides by divine law, whereas the unsuccessful businessman is the person whom worships vanity and abides by the jungle law. Moreover, we were all born for a reason; the divine reason is our business. But to become a successful businessman requires insight and understanding of the divine call. We are all businessmen on earth by reincarnation, but not all of us are successful businessmen by a free will; only when we truly comply with our inner call that we actually become successful businessmen. When we choose our path in life we should ask ourselves whether we took the decision due to faith or due to despair; because faith and despair are the measures of our success and failure. It is because of despair that a man follows the trends of a predatory society to gain power and riches. Hence, the modern businessman is a product of a fallacy. But he who has faith in his true vocation (divine occupation) is a successful businessman regardless of his social class in the world of man. A human society is often plagued by corruptions and therefore it fails to promote the divine occupation. A human society often muffles reason and promotes madness because of the low urge of survivals, and because of fear and worries of the self. But the truth of a man can overcome an entire society despite the consequences, providing that such a man adheres to his divine occupation at all costs. Dear friends, a man who adheres to his spiritual gift is the real businessman. According to the jungle law a successful businessman is the one which society accepts as important due to the jungle law principle of inequality. Adversely, a divine businessman is successful when he serves equality to the full. Friends, we are all businessmen on earth because we all have contracts of reincarnation. Furthermore, we are all part of this socio diversity called life. From the schizophrenic delusional and the deaf to the healthy lawyers and politicians, we are all blessed with the divine seed. The creation of the weak and the strong is the invention of the jungle law devotees. The order of man is destructive when it follows the jungle law. In the divine reality we are all equal occupants with various contracts, but in the system of man equality has been breached and therefore the wicked strong rejoices on the account of the righteous weak. Therefore, dear friends, remember equality and don't ever make any discriminations. If society lives by discriminations and corruptions then you should rebel against society until equality is restored. It might take several generations before the transformation will be completed. Remember, friends, we were born to serve humanity and to give to humanity, not to take from others and not be served by others. Those who believe in the jungle law are members of the underworld, because the jungle law is the heart and fundament of the primitive underworld. The wolf thrives on the thrill of the hunt and on inequality, but the sheep find pastures in the hills of equality.

Comments:

As a child, when I played at my cousin's neighborhood during the holidays, I recall that everybody there wanted to be a successful businessman. There was always something shiny and intriguing about slick businessman, wearing suits and ties and looking so important as if they have all the answers and cures for mankind's deficiencies. However, I was very skeptical as for their spectacle of importance, as I felt that there was also a tinge of arrogance attached to such silent businessmen. 'What is their big secret?' I wondered. The lower class always looked at them in awe and reverence because they were rich and powerful, but I was not convinced that they were the real messengers of society. To have economical security, prestige, and power are natural wants and desires, and there is nothing wrong with such natural wants and desires, however the problem is the shrine that cannot be dismissed. No man can avoid the choice between divine law and the jungle law. No man can ignore the principle of equality, let alone deny it. I recall one businessman in my cousin's neighborhood. Each day, in the evening, when he returned to his home with his suitcase, adults and children alike were whispering in awe about his arrival. Some kids spoke about his success and expressed a wish to become like him some day in the future when they grow up. 'But what does he really do?' I asked them. Then the kids told me, without scruples I might add, for their tone was of respect and pride, that this businessman was selling weapons to big foreign companies. I asked them if they thought it was wrong but they said that they would do the same just to come out of poverty. They spoke about respect for businessmen in general, but completely ignored any morals and ethics in that regard. The transition from infancy to childhood was that in kindergarten most kids dreamt about becoming super heroes, like Superman or Spiderman, but when they evolved to a better understanding of their surroundings, they have suddenly shifted their dream from fiction to non-fiction. Hence now the dream was to become rich and powerful, mostly because of the vain brainwash that comes from parents and society, and not just an imaginary super hero. But when we think about it deeply, it is in fact the opposite that counts. It means that the imaginary dream is analogous to the divine occupation, whereas the mundane dream is analogous to the collective deception which derives from the negative polarity of the jungle law. In other words, what seems unattainable is in fact attainable and vice versa. Yes, no child can become a Superman or a Spiderman, but every child can reach the same level of refinement, hence the same joy and nirvana which accompanies such super heroes. Children dream of becoming superheroes because they wish to feel good and find completion and happiness. But as they grow up from infancy to childhood, they are told that such a refinement is unattainable and that the only way to be happy in this world is by complying with the order of a human society. It means that the dream of the child to find happiness is snapped by the propaganda of the jungle law super organism. The dream, hence, is now shifted from finding happiness in life, to surviving the world of man. But there is no happiness in the world of man because of the distortion of the truth and because of the mass negative consciousness of the jungle law. Here society claims that happiness can be attained by a position of power, or by riches, or by material comfort and prestige, etc. But happiness is an individual find, and salvation is an individual quest. As a poet I often feel the catharsis of a superhero when I create, hence I do not need the lies and compliments of society. Whether rich or poor I have found my inner superhero. I have found my inner businessman and became successful in spirit; whether unemployed or a rich businessman in the physical reality has got no affect on my success as a creative poet. Creativity is my bliss. The prize is spiritual and inner, and the refinery is felt owing to evolution. I adhere to the principle of equality and to the truth that we are on earth to serve and to give. Thus, there is no amount of money, and no position of power that could make me tumble, or tempt me to forsake my inner successful businessman. Furthermore, I have found my inner super hero and now I have rebelled against the madness of a human society, because it misleads. We were born to live, not to survive. We were born to enjoy life, not to suffer the madness of the world. All the oppressions by society that lead to individual depressions and to self destruction stem from the twisted and distorted way society is thinking. The sources of most illnesses are coming from the dogmas of a predatory society, which have vowed to follow the jungle law. The honor is not external, but inner. The real world is the spiritual realm, not the physical reality. Sadly, in many modern societies, a gun dealer, or even a drug dealer, get more respect than modest and humble nurses. Society measures the value of the individual by criteria of possessions, money, and power, with a flagrant disregard to ethics. But from the perspective of equality, we know that the true respect of a human being cannot be genuine without moral virtue. The respect that criminals and corrupted bureaucrats receive in society is false because it is based on inequality (power). I often wonder about the curiosity of children, 'What does your father do?' is a question that some parents would be proud to answer, whereas others will rather remain discreet about. A fireman or a policeman, are still very prestigious occupations in the eyes of children, because of the super hero dream. But the truth is that a nurse, or a doctor, or anyone else who works in service of humanity, is equally important and should be therefore equally respected. However, the elite of society always send signals that they are the most prestigious and most important members of society, because of their high social status and wealth. Money, power, riches, and fame make the dream to be a part of the elite irresistible for anyone who believes in the jungle law. Anyone who adheres to the primitive principle of inequality wishes to be rich and strong like the elites, but such a dream is doomed for the destruction of the human spirit. Anyone who follows inequality is doomed to taste the fruit of vanity, which is a vapor. The real happiness, and the way to salvation, is in the service of society, which is compatible with the spiritual gift. The true vocation is the real promised land of the individual. It is not sufficient to serve society because one is threatened to be cut off social benefits in case one chooses otherwise. It is for the individual to find one's divine occupation, not for society to impose an occupation upon the individual. However, this message also stirred me to feel for the weak in society, for those who are considered as defects in society, are in fact equal businessmen on earth, only that society is too ignorant and too intolerant to fathom their roles on earth. Humanity is superior to society, it means that even a mongoloid, or an autistic person has a divine occupation. Their role is to extract compassion from society. Their weakness and disability is a test of morals for society. They are divine testers, for if society deprives them of their rights, then society failed the test of morals, and hence is classified as a jungle law society. It is wrong for the strong in society to look down at the weak in society. Everyone has a divine task on earth. We all have a reason to be here on earth. The handicap, the mongoloid, the mute, the blind, and everyone else with disability are also a part of human society. Therefore we should never discriminate the weak but on the contrary; we should make a positive change and help them to evolve with their unique needs.

## Emanation XII-    The trees and the refugees

Dear friends, greetings. Only unsound people will disagree with me when I tell you that our planet Earth is on the verge of extinction. Friends, we are nearing a point of no return in regard to the trees. It is by the jungle law aggressive assumption of jurisdiction that some countries allow themselves to destroy the earth. The trees, whose function is highly essential for our very own existence and for the perseverance of the eco system, are cut down to a point whence the forests cannot be restored in the near future. Some trees can live hundreds and even thousands of years, thus when they are chopped down and sold for timber, the loss of their lives is in fact the loss of our oxygen and the loss of our earth. However, the monstrous consciousness of exploitation in regard to the forests is intricately connected with the beastly consciousness of abuse in regard to the lower social class of the refugees. Hence, the refugees in modern Occidental societies are equated with the trees of the great forests. Both the trees and the refugees are victims of the industry that was initiated by the jungle law super organism. The rule of vanity usurps everything which is pure and turns it into a product that serves the higher class in the hierarchy of the jungle law. The unbridled expansion of human habitat, the avaricious extractions of minerals, the decimation of the bees, the mass murder of many marine species, and deforestation are only few of the signs of the earth's destruction. There are two main fronts through which the destruction of the earth takes place. The first front is the physical destruction of the earth, and the second front is the social destruction of human beings. The oppressions and abuse of the lower class in human societies is linked to the exploitations and rape of the earth. When there is no balance within mankind, the earth has got no chance to be healed. When equality is breached within mankind then the extinction of wildlife is marginalized and no one can break the negative vortex of inequality.

Friends, if we wish to heal the earth, we must first heal mankind. The connection between the refugees in Europe and the trees in Siberia is hidden from the world because of the mist of ignorance which clouds the judgment of the general mass. Even in schools and universities the focus of the mainstream is rather on academic achievements than on equality and fairness. The earth is dying, but most people either ignore it or unaware of it. However, the suffering of the earth can only be felt and expressed by the members of the lower classes of society, as they have been subjected to the same misery as of the trees, sharks, and bees. Dear friends, watch out that you do not follow inequality. The fruit of inequality is madness. The selfish ignorant opportunists, who live by the power of madness, money, and riches, are in facts in breach of divine law. The balance of the earth is broken when and individual pledges his legions with inequality. It is by a free will and by convictions of a person that the destruction of the earth begins. The nucleus of the general mass is either equality or inequality. Sadly, the jungle law rules the general mass of mankind, and the solidarity of the selfish criminals usurped the solidarity of the chaste altruists. But we can reverse it, dear friends, by telling the next generations the truth about the nature of mankind. We have the choice to rebel against destruction. We can break the jungle law and reinforce divine law. We can create environmental laws that will safeguard the trees and wildlife. We can improve the lives of domesticated animals, prohibit industrial chickens, prohibit abuse of animals, and restore human rights. We can safeguard the refugees and protect them from the harm of the jungle law worshippers in all worldwide societies. Dear friends, rebel against people who destroy the earth. Furthermore, dissociate yourselves from the avaricious jungle law extremists whose agenda is to thrive on the spoils of material comfort. The real pot of gold in the end of the rainbow is equality. Find equality and you will taste salvation. The jungle law worshippers only follow the material world. Moreover, they only take care of their own social status, thus they ignore the pain of the weak in society as if the weak does not exist. It is the same with the trees of the earth; these trees and forests are part of our eco system. Friends, we all share the same planet, and everything that we do has an affect on all of us. The negative consciousness of inequity is growing exponentially among people because of selfishness and greed. Those who ignore deforestation and those who ignore the madness of discrimination in society, are only adding fuel to the fire of the earth's destruction. The total destruction of the earth is a result of apathy and ignorance. Fools claim that it is not their problem that the earth is dying or that the lower class is suffering. The predatory rabble is dumb enough to think that the oppression of the refugees and the deforestation of the trees is not part of their daily problem. But the truth is that the ignorance, apathy, and greed of the general mass are in fact serving the agenda of the jungle law super organism. Dear friends, we must unite against the destruction of the earth and rebel against the violations of human rights. Our solidarity is based on the fact that the earth belongs to all of us, and to all other species in peace and social harmony. Bio diversity is the earth's beauty and health. Dear friends, each and every single individual in the world bear the responsibility to take care of the earth and protect it. The earth is precious and fragile, and its bio, eco, and socio systems are inseparable. Dear friends, the jungle law aggressive principle of territorialism is a lie, for the earth belongs to everybody. Furthermore, territorialism and jurisdictions should neither undermine nor weaken the principles of peace and social harmony. No country has the right to destroy big forests. We are equal in share, dear friends, so let us heal the earth and restore it to its former beauty and glory. It is the choice of predatory mankind to break equality and create social statuses that destroys society and the earth. But our choice, dear friends, is to heal the earth, to restore human rights, and to restore equality. Our choice is subversive of the jungle law. We choose to topple down the jungle law and usurp it by the introduction and promotion of divine law. Therefore, dear friends, we should aspire towards equality and towards the preservation of the forests at the same time. The link here is in care, love, fairness, and equality. We are triggered by peace consciousness, not by war consciousness and therefore we must change the law of man so that it will be compatible with divine law and not with the jungle law. A human being has no right to degrade and oppress nature. A human being has no right to oppress and exploit another human being. Dear friends, we are all equal in worth. A country has no right to fell trees in its assumed territories, and a society has no right to kill or oppress a human being in its assumed physical reality. Friends, life is a test, please don't fail it. Stay loyal to divine law and to the principles of salvation. Set the refugees free from the claws of human society. Remain faithful to peace and love, and make a stop to the madness of deforestation.

Poem:                    Unfree

The refugee is like a tree,
That has been cut down;
He has no country, no roots,
His share was stolen from him;
His soul was chopped to pieces,
And he was sold by the industry;
The material comforters bought him,
To be burnt in their homes' furnace;
Where a human society thrives,
On the fiery lake of hell.

The tree was cut down for its beauty,
And for its use for paper;
The forests begin to disappear,
The green is gone, oxygen is rare;
Opportunism destroyed the forests,
Avarice made many birds homeless;
Like the refugees, the homes of birds,
Were looted and destroyed.

The time has come to restore the forests,
The time has come to plant tress;
The time has come to restore justice,
The time has come to restore human rights;
The time has come to revive equality.

Justice is like a green forest that was cut down,
Inequality is like deforestation;
It undermines the foundations of society,
And tarnishes the majesty of the earth;
Trees are like divine human beings,
They breathe and feel and love;
And the refugee is like a tree,
Innocent like the earth, unfree;
Cut down, in pain, unfree,
Unfree.

Comments:

Due to my own personal experience in exile, I have felt the pain of the earth and the pain of the weak in society all the time. Often I thought about the hearing of dogs, as they can hear whistles and audio frequencies which humans cannot hear. Their hearing sense is far more developed and advanced than ours. For me, such an enhanced sense was the sense of care for the earth. Many times when I felt the pain of the weak in society I was met with hollow faces, as most people either did not care about the pain of the weak, or that they just were not really aware of it. Some were even entertained by it. My published poetry, together with my other literary works consolidates my theory that poets are the true moral leaders of mankind. Most of the survivalists in my generation were opportunists whom were focusing only on the prize of the prey and on the carcasses of material comfort and money. The lottery winner was the hero of society not the divine messenger. Hence, rich people were the heroes of the masses because of the rabble's devotion to the jungle law. As a poet I felt that it was the end of civilization, chiefly since evolution was forbidden because of the rule of vanity. However, like other sheep I lived by equality and observed the pain of the weak in society. Thereupon, I vowed to help the weak and heal the earth. Helping the weak in society on my behalf was out of compassion, not out of a convention or a social trend. In that context I was a non conformist and a rebel because the weak were the enemy in society. I rebelled thus against primitivism owing to my rebellion against the madness of opportunism. The refugees in Denmark were demonized by the media but I knew the truth that their role was to stand as a moral test for society. The trees in Siberia, Indonesia, Sweden, Brazil, and Canada, were also my trees, even though I was born in Israel. My concern was for the entire planet, earth, as I was devoted to altruism. I understand that it is not easy to fathom the connection between the refugees and the trees of the earth, but I believe that in this emanation I have succeeded in bringing the mind of the reader closer to the truth of our destruction. We were not born to live by the jungle law; we were born to revive divine law. Deforestation must be stopped by law and by compassion. The abuse of the refugees must be stopped by law and by compassion. Equality is the key factor in the restoration of divine order.

# Emanation XIII:    Being lost and being found

Dear friends, who among us is lost and who among us is found? Do
you know? Those who are found in the system of man are lost in the
kingdom of heaven, because the system of man is governed by the rule
of power. Friends, there is no way around it, for conformism to the
jungle law, or adaptation to the reality which is dictated and governed
by the jungle means in fact waywardness. The true way to salvation
means conformism to divine law and to moral virtue, not to madness
and power. Therefore, anyone who chooses to conform to power, war,
opportunism, primitivism, and inequality is lost. But anyone who
chooses to conform to chastity, peace, altruism, ethics, and equality is
in fact found in salvation, and the spirit of serenity is within him.
Remember, dear doves, we construct in the spirit all the time. Due to
motion we are bound either to evolve or to go backwards, though with
the ever chance to sway and alter our paths and destinies. Hence,
there is hope even for criminals to change in life. My advice here is to
walk always in the positive path of moral virtue, because only in the
positive (+1, Yang chi) path there is a growth in salvation. In fact, we
cannot remain on point zero. Thus, if we are not positive then we are
negative, and that means that a man who is not found in salvation is
in fact lost. A man who is found is like a ship that found the golden
shore of salvation. But a man who is lost is like a ship that sails
endlessly in a stormy sea. Either a man is safe and sound or that he is
lost in faith. It is faith and despair that determine whether we are lost
or found in life. Dear friends, when people are mocking you and
humiliate you, do not pay attention to them. The most important
thing here is that you do not join them in mockery. Do not ever join
the jungle law, because it is the negative polarity of the lost. Stay out of
inequality and do not sit in the assembly of mockers. Do not exploit
others for money. Rebel against the madness of the predatory
opportune; do not join it. Dear doves, this generation is not only cruel

and retarded, indifferent and vain, it is also a lost generation that destroys the earth without scruples. Watch out for this dark generation and its destructive ways. Money and material comfort are not the way to salvation; they are the way to destruction. If you will follow money and material comfort, then you will remain forever lost. Instead, follow your true call in life through moral virtue. Because those who follow their spiritual call and gift are strong in faith, and when they apply moral virtue in everything that they do, then they are found in salvation and they will never be lost as long as they remain loyal to their true call through ethics. Dear doves, walk only in the positive way and abide by the law of the dove. Those who follow divine law are already found by faith. Dear friends, a positive seed will grow to a positive tree, and a positive tree will yield a positive fruit. The fruit of salvation comes from the seed of salvation. The seed of salvation is divine law, hence all those who follow their divine call on earth and abide by divine law are found in salvation. Dear doves; that is why it is important that you choose the right path of faith. Do not associate yourselves with corrupt societies, and do not befriend yourselves with selfish predators who worship the jungle law. Stay away from the crooked ways that lead to crime and dishonor. Stay away from the lost that intend to harm you. Like lepers the lost can affect you with ignorance and apathy that stems from the jungle law. Deplore and shun vanity, dear doves. Stay faithful to salvation and remain only positive. Those who are lost are the killers of the earth, but those who are found are the healers of the earth.

Comments:

It is important for me to remark here that not all the lost are
intentionally destructive. One can be lost because of naivety and
innocence. However, the criticism here is against the lost who are lost
out of a free will to follow the jungle law. There are two chief
categories of the lost, which are associated with the spheres of the Yin
-1 and the zero. The innocent lost (0, Sha) are folks whom are
unaware of the truth of what is going on in life, whereas the wicked
lost (-1, Yin) are folks who vowed to serve the jungle law and follow
inequality. Hence, this message was not meant to alienate the reader
from others, but rather instruct to be aware of the degrees of
evolution. When I met innocent lost people I have always tried to help
them as a matter of principle, but when I have encountered wicked
lost folks it was my principle to avoid them. The wicked lost are in fact
found in vanity (world of man) and therefore they are depicted as
wicked in this message. Examples for wicked lost are bankers who
steal from their customers, or doctors who deliberately make money
on their patients without regard as for their victims' health, or lawyers
that dismiss justice and only care about to win a case for the sake of
their ego. Therefore, we should be warned here, to watch out for
radical approaches. Take the mild approach and give everyone a
chance to be your friend. But when you feel that a person is rotten
because of the jungle law, then it is better to dissociate oneself from
such a person. Judge only by the taste of the fruit, and not by the
external appearance of it; watch out for prejudice. Be open and fair,
and give the lost a chance to be found. The reason I brought up this
message here has also to do with the massive brainwash of the
individual by a primitive society, as here one is considered found
when one conforms to the order and system of society. It is better to
be a homeless than to surrender one's spiritual gift and conform to the
madness of a jungle law society. It is better to starve in the body than

to become a predator in the spirit, because when a man surrenders his soul to the system of man, he becomes lost in the kingdom of heaven.

Emanation XIV:   The real home

Greetings, dear doves; peace and love upon you. During our lives we establish our spiritual structures. Some people invest everything in their divine call; hence, their properties are analogous to big mansions and luxurious estates. Those who invest less have their homes in a modest fashion, with sufficient place in which to dwell in peace. However, those who do not invest at all in their spiritual gifts are in fact homeless in the spiritual realm. Paradoxically, on earth we are often confounded by the illusion that it is the complete opposite. Dear friends, anyone who follows the jungle law is homeless in the divine realm. On earth the jungle law elites, i.e. the rich and famous, have twisted the truth and assumed property in accordance with the predatory principles of power, greed, and selfishness. Often such properties are shrouded by the atmosphere of spiritual death, emptiness, hollowness, and dullness. We should ask ourselves the question, 'What does the rich property owner really achieve in living in such a big mansion without any form of a happy life?' I tell you the truth; happiness can only come from the achievements in the divine order. A rich man's goals are based on inequality, but the goals of a divine law follower, regardless of his social status or abundance of possessions, are based on equality, and therefore the prize of such a man is true happiness. The real home is not in the vanities of the physical world. The real home is where the heart is, where faith is, aye where salvation is. Love is the real home. Peace is the real home, equality is the real home. Therefore, dear doves, build your homes in the spirit. Any person that follows his/her spiritual call has a home, because salvation is the kingdom of the found. But any person that betrays salvation and chooses to follow the whims and quirks of the jungle law is in fact a homeless, because vanity is the kingdom of the lost. If you love the world and hate life, then you are homeless, but if you love life and despise the vanities of the world, then you have a home in the heavenly realm, and the size of your home is in accordance with your merits, achievements, and devotion to the truth of your divine contract on earth. Fairness is the indicator of your path. Be fair and follow the divine contract. Abide by divine law and your wealth will grow and grow exponentially. Dear doves, the real home of a human being is unseen, because it is a spiritual abode. Do not be fooled by the jungle law worshippers whom are proud of their property on earth. Their agenda serves inequality, and because of their infatuations with inequality, power, and pride, they have removed themselves from salvation and became homeless in the heavenly realm. The fallacy of the mundane world, or the madness of the physical reality, affected many people to a point of unrelenting selfishness. But anyone who is consumed by selfishness in faith is bound to have no home in the spiritual world. Because selfishness that serves inequality is rewarded by the jungle law, and not by divine law. The rewards of the jungle law are the illusions of material comfort, pride, power, and possessions. Moreover the essence of these rewards is homelessness, destruction, and spiritual death. The home of life is divine law. Dear friends, the consciousness of the jungle law followers is analogous to the destructive phenomena of splitting atoms. The System of Man is a system of destruction that is similar to the splitting atoms of a spiritual life. Human rights are violated systematically because of the rule of vanity in society. The jungle law super organism systematically decimates divine needs, human rights, animal's rights, nature, and everything pure in life. Examine the truth of reality, dear doves, for greed, apathy, selfishness, ignorance and all what the ego produces derives from the negative polarity of vanity. The destruction of our world is a result of the destruction of life. The worship of vanity undermines the existence of salvation. Evolution itself has become extinct because of the industry that stems from the system of man. Dear friends, the real home is not earth. The real home is within us, it is Love. The real home is heaven. Heaven is within us.

Comments:

The warning in many of my messages is to watch out for social brainwash. The progress of a human being is not real when it is dictated by the system of man, because the system of man is influenced by the jungle law. In Denmark the madness of property was often promoted by a massive brainwash that came from the media. Here an individual was subjected to the propaganda which stated that material comfort is far more important than human rights. There were many points in my life in which I could join the masses in pursuit of comfort, money, and power, but I felt that it was wrong, and therefore never took the broad road which leads to self destruction. Despite the temptations I have rebelled against the mainstream and chose the narrow path which leads to salvation. I have found my real home in poetry, and I have no doubt in my mind that had I was blessed with another spiritual gift, that I would have followed it as well. My low social status in exile enabled me to help the weak because I was subjected to the same hardships and misery. Often in the messages I felt, as a reader, that there was a melancholy drift, yet not unjustified. The drift may seem negative but the messages are always positive. I must admit here that I am not a pessimist but simply a disillusioned realist who watches planet earth dies right before me. The apathy, sadism, and ignorance of the multitudes only serve vanity and add to the self destruction of both the human spirit and planet earth. In the system of man which is based on vanity, and on its jungle law, people always told me: 'If you are not happy over there come and live here' as if they owned the earth. In some places one was told, 'We don't like you here, don't live here. Go to another country' as if people own the world, the earth, and even the universe. However, I was very skeptical as for the authenticity of such claims, because I knew that we are only mortal. No human being can outlive the earth, let alone own it. I have found it very strange that mankind had everything divided to territories and to properties, etc. Often it wrongly felt as if it was their world and that I was just a guest in it because I was following the law of salvation. Gradually I have ignored the spokesmen of the jungle law and found serenity havened in the truth within me. The world does not belong to anyone, for we are only guests here with tasks and errands. Anyone who derails or stray from the truth of his/her mission on earth, follows by thus inequality. The truth is that the world belongs to everyone, not only to humans. Those who follow the truth of social harmony, bio diversity, and a perfect eco system are followers of equality. Such persons should be praised not condemned. Thus, I always felt that the Greenpeace members in Scandinavia were hypocrites because their phony zealous love towards the environment could not compensate as for their genuine zealous hatred towards foreigners. It is enough that there is intolerance in regard to humans to destroy the delicate balance of equality. At the same length those who work for human rights in Asia become offenders of divine law when they break the balance of equality each time they order a fin shark soup in a restaurant. The balance of equality is as delicate as it is perfect, thus, we should aspire to restore equality both in regard to a human society and in regard to the environment. I should also remark here that a man is not born (destined) to live somewhere or to own something. We are not on earth to settle down, for we are not the kings of the earth. We are not the landlord, we are merely the tenants, or rather guests of honor on a short visit. Planet earth is a hotel which we do not own. A man is born to serve others, or to complete something that serves others. A man's home is in his service, and in his divine occupation, and in his passions towards his spiritual gift. Good deeds are the foundations of the heavenly house. Personally, I feel that without my poetry I would have surely been a homeless in both worlds. A man in service should welcome positive invitations to live somewhere when invited, but it should be in accordance with his service, and not for the goal of survival or vanity. The madness of the lost begins with the search for vanity. The shrine of vanity is an illusion built on a quicksand. To live somewhere out of fear or concern of becoming a homeless is an absurd. Survivals are not the goal. Happy spiritual life is the goal. However, pragmatism is also an exception to divine law, for life is the highest goal, not death. However, it is not the pragmatic mundane choice but rather the creed which is the issue here; because anyone who hibernates in the consciousness of vanity is lost. Material comfort, money, and power, and everything that stems from predatory opportunity lead to homelessness in the heavenly realm. Therefore we should never focus on such nonsense as material things, but rather focus on the human experience and achievements in regard to our spiritual evolution. Dear friends, do not live in such a base consciousness that promotes material comfort. Instead, live by the true call in your life and by your true service. You can find salvation even if you are homeless on earth. Your true vocation is far more powerful than the physical reality. I wish to conclude the comments here with the declaration that humankind's biggest challenge in life is not to harm the earth. The test of morals is hanging on the thin threads of fairness and equality.

## Emanation XV:     The parable of the plants

Once there was a group of inmates in a correctional facility whom one day were visited by a farmer who lectured them about his orchards and plantations. The farmer then gave the prisoners some of his fruits and implied that the wise ones among the prisoners will be rewarded if they'd known what to do with the fruits. Time has passed and it appeared that most of the prisoners just ate the fruits, thereupon disposed of the fruits' leftovers and seeds. Nevertheless, very few inmates kept the seeds of the fruits; thereupon planted them in small pots and plastic cups which were placed by their narrow barred windowed. Thus, they watered the seeds and allowed rays of sunlight to shine upon the seeds. When the seeds sprouted out slowly, the inmates followed their growth. It gave them hope and joy. However, when few more years passed the inmates were faced with a problem. Their plants could not grow taller because of the walls and ceilings of their prison cells. The need for more soil and for open air made everyone realize that the big fruit plants now will not survive prison and that they must return to nature or wither. The wardens called the farmer to come and pick up the new trees. However, when the farmer came to visit, he also requested some workers to help him with his orchards and plantations. He requested the help of inmates who cared about trees. Shortly after the application forms were sent away, the wardens received permission from their superiors to let the farmer employ some of the inmates on a daily basis. When the farmer had to choose his workers he chose the inmates whom let the seeds grow. The few inmates who cherished the seeds were delighted to work in nature. From that day on they have spent all day in a free environment, in a cordial nice atmosphere in nature whence they picked up fruits during the summer and took care of the trees all year long. The farmer was so pleased with their work that he recommended their return to society, so that they could work with him in nature. Owing to the good recommendations of the farmer, his workers were released sooner from prison. Thus, when they were free he employed them like other decent equal member of society, with full wages and rights as everybody else. Few years later they were privileged to share land, plant their own trees, and harvest fruits for themselves and for their families.

Comments:

The lesson here is the same with regard to salvation. Dear friends, we are all analogous to the inmates on earth, because we are confined by the physical reality on one hand and by the rule of vanity on the other hand. During our lives we dream about spiritual freedom and total happiness, and about perfection. The seeds in this message are analogues to the divine seeds, which are known as the spiritual gifts. Once more, I should give my own example that if I did not cherish the gift of poetry, I would have never found inner peace and inner happiness. The spiritual gift is the seed of salvation, thus, after I have given my spiritual gift the right conditions and allowed it to prosper and grow, I have managed to harvest it and taste salvation. There is no amount of money and no degree of fame that can sway me from my spiritual gift of poetry. Poverty and wealth are totally irrelevant here, because the spiritual gift triumphs over the physical reality. In the above parable, the inmates that disposed of the fruits' seeds are analogous to people who threw their spiritual gifts to the garbage. Such a fatal mistake often occurs when power, money, material comfort, vain pride, and other vanities cloud the judgment of a person and tempt one to follow the jungle law. Had I chosen to conform to modern society, I would have to yield my gift of poetry because of the transition to the jungle law. The consciousness of war and power decimates the seeds of salvation; hence a human being cannot live in two consciousnesses. Think about fresh water fish, if you'd move them to the ocean they will not survive. Examine the suffering and cruel death of the salmon when they return from the oceans to the fresh water rivers in order to spawn. Shortly after they spawn they die a painful death because they cannot adapt to the new environment. It is the same with a man who works in the system of the jungle law super organism. Such a person cannot adapt to society unless he disposed of his seeds of salvation. Because society is based on vanity, and vanity do not tolerate salvation. Thus, power decimates beauty because of the choice of society to follow the jungle law. Often artists express their views against bureaucrats and politicians by criticizing them for their heartless attitudes. The conformers to a jungle law society are often described as robots, automatons, machines, and inhuman. Such harsh criticism is both veracious and justified, since all conforms to a jungle law society are equated with the inmates who chose to dispose of the fruits' seeds. Dear friends, do not ever give up your dreams of evolution. Do not ever dispose of your spiritual gifts. Do not ever ignore the seeds of salvation. The wisest of all people are those whom nurture their spiritual gifts and follow their divine call on earth. The foolish of all people are those who ignore their divine contracts, and reject their spiritual gifts. The physical reality is a deception that tempts many people to follow the jungle law. Dear friends, I urge you to follow your hopes and dreams, and to rebel against ignorant societies. If you wish to be found in salvation, and live free and happy in salvation, then do not ever toss the seeds of your spiritual gifts away. Keep the divine seeds in a safe place, thereupon nurture them and let them grow. Give the divine seeds the climates they need, for one day the farmer will come for a visit and he will redeem all those who remained faithful to the seeds of salvation.

## Emanation XVI:   The parable of the two drunkards

Once there were two drunkards whom met in a festival. They were drinking, each their own special made wine, until they got really drunk. Then they were staring at each other's wine and wondering about the taste of it. One was drinking a red wine, whereas the other was drinking a white wine. They were both happy for their wines and claimed that it was the source of their happiness. Curiosity led them to a strange conversation. The man who drank white wine asked the man who drank red wine: 'What kind of wine are you drinking, friend? And why is it red?' At that his fellow drunkard replied: 'This is not an ordinary wine, stranger. This is the wine of the wolf. It is red from the blood of war, and it was made out of the grapes of inequality, power, and rage. Once you have tasted this wine and you will become a leader of war that wins every battle'. At that both drunkards were laughing out loud, as it was not clear whether the reply was meant in a trifle humor or in a grave sincerity. Then the man who drank red wine asked the man who drank white wine: 'What kind of wine are you drinking, stranger? And why is it transparent?' At that his fellow drunkard replied: 'This is a very ordinary wine, friend. It is the crystal clear white wine of peace. This is the wine of the white dove, and it is made out of grapes of fairness, equality, and harmony. Once you have tasted this wine and you will become a shepherd of peace that leads many herds to green pastures'. At that both drunkards were laughing out loud, as it was not clear whether the reply was meant in a trifle humor or in a grave sincerity. Then the man who drank red wine asked his fellow drunkard: 'May I taste from the wine of the dove?' The man who drank white wine nodded and poured his wine in a cup and rendered it to his fellow drunkard. 'That is a horrible wine, how can you drink it?' exclaimed the red wine drunkard after he tasted from the white wine. However, when the white wine drunkard tasted the red wine he expressed the same view. Thus, they both agreed that they disapproved of each other's taste of wine, and that it was acceptable to dislike each other's wine. They laughed at each other, and laughed with each other, and drank more and more wine. Thereupon, they were engrossed with expressionism that had its source in their wines. The dove-wine drunkard suddenly recited poetry and spoke about carpe diem and about the beauties of life. The wolf-wine drunkard cursed life and spoke about death and destruction, money and possessions, and about other vanities. Then they have confessed about their deeds in accordance with their wines and laughed. 'I have saved many souls' exclaimed the white wine drunkard and added, 'I have worked as a healer, and healed many sick people for many years'. Then the red wine drunkard confessed, 'I have killed many people in wars' and added, 'Later I worked in a mafia and tortured many people to death'. 'You have a great sense of humor' said the white wine drunkard to the red wine drunkard. 'It is all true' admitted the red wine drunkard, but his fellow drunkard was in doubt, and they were both laughing. Then they were hugging and singing, staggering about with their wine. Then the white wine drunkard invited the red wine drunkard to his home. When they entered the house in which the white wine drunkard lived the red wine drunkard became very crazy and violent. He grabbed an axe and murdered his fellow drunkard. Thereupon he fell asleep next to the dead drunkard. When the wife and the children of the white wine drunkard returned home in the morning, they have found their beloved one dead on the floor. Their cries of pain woke up the red wine drunkard who now tied the children and locked them up in another room. Then he raped the wife of the dead drunkard and drank more red wine. When he sobered up he took the children and their mother to the market place and sold them as slaves to a rich merchant. Afterwards he sold the house of his fellow dead drunkard, and with the money that he earned he traveled to the next festival. But few weeks later, in a tavern, he was sitting next to another drunkard and told him the story. However, it appeared that the drunkard who sat next to him and laughed all the time was just a local fool who loved to drink water from a bottle wine. Then the truth was found out about the atrocious crimes of the red wine drunkard. Thereupon he was caught by the law and sentenced to a lifetime in prison.

Comments:

This parable reminds me so much about the two different mentalities and consciousnesses of Israel and Denmark. The horrible reciprocity that I have experienced, and which other hundreds of people have experienced are mirrored in the above parable. The way a human being is always treated as a stranger and as an enemy in Scandinavia, because of the imposed war against individualism, puzzled me at first, as I was brought up in a kibbutz, as here the way a human being was treated was completely the opposite. The mentality of murder in Denmark, hence the suicides, the homicides, and the overflowing crimes have a source in the wine of the jungle law. Such a wine is a consciousness and a spirit, and often I wondered: how could people rejoice at the fall and misery of others? Later to realize that I was very fortunate to be born in the miracle that was once called Israel. The give and the take principle has been both distorted and abused as here what Israel gave as a society to a foreign individual was in fact robbed away from any individual in Denmark. All the values of salvation, like love, peace, fairness, equality, human and natural rights, were systemically murdered by the Danish system. The right to laugh, the right to think, the right to feel, the right live, among many other rights and liberties, were all oppressed by the consciousness of murder of the human spirit in Denmark. It was upon the wine of death, with which the Scandinavian masses are intoxicated, that vanity rules and crime thrives. Thus, I felt that this parable was accurate in its advocacy for all individuals in Denmark in general, but for foreigners in particular. This parable also reminded me that the truth in Denmark is suppressed by the sober, yet expressed by the drunkard. The norm of speaking the truth in public for the drunkard is a mystery to a stranger. The sad fact is that the truth is not allowed to have an expression in public, unless spoken by a drunkard, for then the rabble is amused. Often the encroachment upon private life occurs because of the imposition not to feel free and not to speak the truth freely in society, as the truth is in fact considered a hazard for the structure of Danish society. All the material riches and fortunes of Denmark were hoarded owing to lies and owing to the manifestations of human corruptions that are methodically concealed. Even the myriads of murders, hence the homicides and suicides, which are plaguing Denmark are marginalized by the media. In fact the mentality of murder in Denmark is wearing the guise of a stealthy kindness. Thus, all the evil that is happening is in fact usurped by the agenda of riches and material comfort. Hence, the talk of the day is focused on the rich jungle law alpha leaders of society, whereas the lower class is oppressed, mutilated, suffocated, and silenced. Danish society has decided that a human being has no worth, and that, furthermore, the only measure of the value of a human being is in accordance with one's social class and abundance of wealth. Personally, I have felt betrayed for twenty years, as I have experienced hell in a foreign society whose children received heaven by my own society. My society gave love, freedom, and life to thousands of Danish individuals, whereas Denmark rendered me with hatred, illness, and death. However, I was not the only one, as many other foreigners from moral societies found themselves in the reality of a spiritual death in Denmark. Basically, the wine of salvation (carpe diem) is the Yang Chi wine of peace and creativity, whereas the wine of vanity (hatred of life) is the Yin Chi wine of war and destruction. Hence, the culture shock of foreigners in Denmark suggests an explanation as for the adaptation of some foreigners to the madness of Danish society, whereas others cannot adapt because of the jungle law. A man can drink either a Yang wine or a Yin wine, and by such a choice of wine, hence become intoxicated with either life or death; with either love or hatred; with either war or peace. The love of life and the love of the world are two violent contrasts that nobody can ignore. The one who loves life despises the material world, because the material world is the lethal fruit of vanity. The one who loves the world loathes life itself, because life is the peaceful fruit of salvation. A man cannot live both in peace and in war within himself. In the scales of balance, the one who loves life hates the world, whereas the one who loves the world hates life. To which scale the balance of justice will be tilted is a matter of personal faith, but no one can deceive destiny. Those who are intoxicated on the wine of the love of life will be rewarded with Nirvana, whereas those who are intoxicated on the wine of the love of the world will be rewarded with futility. The additional message here is not to trust the jungle law followers. Here I have felt the same betrayal by Danish society when I invited it to my home: chastity. Here I was spiritually murdered, like many other foreigners, by Danish society. I was fool enough to serve a Danish herd, not realizing that it was not a herd of sheep but in reality a herd of swine. The fact that I have worked for so many years in Denmark and contributed to a better society rendered me with spiritual death, depressions, and ever lasting misery. Not only that I have been exploited, mocked, stolen from, harassed, degraded, mistreated, and emotionally abused, but I have also been subjected to the murder of my spiritual gift. However, after I have realized the truth about the reality of the jungle law in Denmark, I have found refuge in my poetry. As human beings we are bound to choose out wine in life, either the wine of vanity or the wine of salvation. Thus, I was intoxicated with love because I have chosen the wine that was made out of the vines and grapes of my spiritual gift. The physical reality was just a test of faith. I knew that I have passed the test when I was drunk on the wine of Nirvana and carpe diem. However, I have learned an important lesson, which is never to drink wine next to people who drink from the wine of the jungle law.

Emanation XVII:   The Alpha Artist

Peace, dear doves, and greetings to you from the spiritual desert of exile. Equality is a personal choice, not a political system and not a social system, for equality is a spirit not a human constitution. Friends, like all others in society some artists believe and live in the noble and wonderful notion of equality whereas others believe and live in the madness of jungle law. But I tell you the truth; a real artist cannot live by both laws: jungle and divine. A true artist cannot live by the jungle law for then he/she is not an artist, for artists are the opposite of predatory opportunists. Anyone who follows the jungle law rule of power and/or aspires for the prizes of material comfort, money, and vain pride is in a fact the opposite of an artist. Modesty and honesty are the traits of a true artist. Hence, when an artist chooses to remain loyal to divine law; such an artist becomes real and genuine. The loyalty of the artist to divine law is through moral virtue, reason, and through all the principles of salvation. When an artist breaks the balance of fairness and equality and chooses to become disloyal to his true call/vocation, then he is in fact a wolf in sheep clothing. The transformation from a loyal artist to a disloyal artist occurs when selfishness and inequality are adopted by the artist. An artist has to choose between selflessness and selfishness, thus it is by the choice of the artist's heart that he is valued, and not by his artistic works, or by his merits. In fact, an artist is denuded of the divine title 'Artist' when he chooses to abide by the jungle law. The artist disgraces his spiritual gift, tarnishes it, and even abuses it when he chooses to sell his soul to the polarity of vanity. In the hierarchy of the jungle law it happens that the Alpha artist is the epitome of both selfishness and industrialism. Real artists do not create in order to make money, for real artists are divine artists that create because of a message, because of a vision, because of a meaning, hence, because of evolution.   Real artists do not create in order to become famous, for real artists create out of a divine purpose to share their vision with mankind. Real artists do not create because they worship the self, they create because the serve the selfless. In the order of the sheep, equality, there is no alpha leader. Here all members of the herd are equal, and they are all modest in the service of the divine order. It is the jungle law that has created the alpha leader because of the principle of inequality. There is an order of a pack of wolves in which the alpha leader is superior to everyone else. Therefore, an artist cannot be both an artist and an alpha leader. The term alpha artist, hence, is a paradox, and by thus it becomes obsolete and subsequently void and null. When an artist chooses to follow the jungle law then he is no longer an artist but just another opportunistic predator.

Comments:

In this emanation I have come to think about the industry of films, books, theater, and culture as a whole. The most common temptation which is offered to an individual by the jungle is the temptation of survivals. Many artists sold themselves to the system of man and became slaves of the jungle law money industry. I thought about film writers and screen writers as the biggest slaves of the jungle law. The choice whether to become a slave of the jungle law or a servant of divine law is a matter of spiritual life and spiritual death. The authors who write in order to make money, or in order to become famous, or in order to promote themselves, or even in order to survive have chosen the broad road of spiritual death. The destruction of the human spirit begins with the industrialization and systematization of all pure things. A survival is used as a pretext here, because survivals are not genuine when it becomes an industry. If a man has got nothing to eat and he hunts a deer in the forest then he is not in violation of divine law because here the exception of survivals serves salvation. Here, the exception is real and genuine. But when a man makes an industry out of deer and sells deer meat and deer skin to the world market, then he is in violation of divine law, because here his industry serves vanity and destruction. When artists create for the sake of evolution, then they are real, pure, chaste, and divine, for evolution serves salvation, but when artists create for the sake of material comfort, selfishness, and for the sake of any other foul motive then they are not real artists, but rather opportunistic predators, and we can call them alpha artists. Art is either a call or a fall. Art is a call when an artist is faithful as for the message of his art, whereas art is a fall when an artist betrays his true call, and instead he wanders off to find riches, fame, and other vanities with his art. The jungle law is a deception; predatory realism is an illusion. The real life of a human being takes place in the divine realism. Sadly, many artists chose to yield to inequality because of the mass collective consciousness of those who are infatuated with the jungle law. When we observe the alpha male in nature, or the alpha female of any pack of wild animals, we learn that they are addicted to the jungle law. They are infatuated with power and pride. Selfishness is the core power of the jungle law. Territorialism, possessions, and pride are emphasized among the alpha leaders of the pack. Moreover, the alpha leaders enjoy prerogatives that break the balance of fairness and equality. In many packs it is the alpha male that enjoys sex with the females, while all the other males in the pack are deprived of such a natural need. It is the same with rich people in a human society; they allow themselves to be spoiled rotten on the account of many exploited and deprived poor people. The saddest part here is that often the under class admire the rich alpha leaders of society because of their wealth and power. Sadly, many people believe in the system of inequality. Furthermore, many people follow the spirit of inequality and worship the power of the jungle law. Although I gave this example about artists, it should be remarked here that it is also the actual/relevant case in all occupations of society. When we adopt the spiritual gift and follow moral virtue, love, equality, and reason, then our occupation is a divine occupation. However, when we betray our spiritual gift and follow power, greed, money, and inequality, then our occupation is a primitive predatory occupation. We can decide whether our occupation belongs with the order of the angel (salvation) or with the order of the beast (vanity). To choose to become an alpha artist means to become a predatory artist. Here, just like doctors, dentists, lawyers, and politicians an artist is bound to opt between the temptations/lies of the jungle law, and the truth of divine law. When one is denuded form the sphere of morality, one severs the balance of the whole. The collapse of a human being begins with the elimination of the middle sphere, which is ethics. Hence, many times we hear about corrupt lawyers whom are criminals in the guise of decent lawyers, or about underworld primitive societies in the guise of civilized high societies. The warning here is not to go astray. As artists we have an important role, thus we must keep our faith and never betray our true call to serve the truth of our errand. Writers and authors choose the jungle law out of despair because of the oppression of human beings in society. The dog snarls and marks his territory, and it has no tolerance towards others in the pack, unless he is overpowered. Such famous rich authors behave in our modern society. They have betrayed everyone, including themselves because they have chosen the path of selfishness, jealousy, competitions, and war. Dear friends, when you are envious at others then you are shrouded by darkness, and there is no salvation within you. In truth, every artist knows his own purity of heart. Do not judge others and do not drink from contaminated rivers, like the incorporated media, but know the nature of one another without passing judgment. Help others if help is needed. Equality or inequality, and hostility or affinity are daily dilemmas, so make the right choice and stay faithful to the order of the dove. As a personal example I have expressed the guidance to rebel against selfishness, pride, and competitions in the book 'The solidarity of poets'. Finally, I should praise J.D Salinger here for his faithfulness, and for his devotion to divine law. Despite of his lack of artistic beauty in regard to his literary works, and despite of the fact that he was an aficionado of literature and pure message rather than a real author, he did not yield to the industry of the jungle law. He is the perfect example of a real artist.

Emanation XVIII:    Vengeance vs. Justice


Dear friends, be careful when you pursue justice and make sure that you do not follow the primitive law of the jungle when you intend for justice to prevail. Seeking justice and seeking revenge is not the same thing. He who seeks justice lives in peace and serenity within himself, but he who seeks revenge lives at war within himself and has no cure and no remedy. Dear doves, the slight difference between justice and vengeance is expressed through actions not through words. Do not ever retaliate, and do not wash your hands with blood, for the law of the dove stands against crime. Also in cases of teasing and provocation, you should not retaliate, although on many occasions the temptation to intervene and restore peace and balance is too great. Friends, when a man is provoking you and pushing you to your limits one has the free will to leave it be and ignore that man. But in cases when the options to leave the place and ignore the provocateur are nullified you should seek the help of another rational human being and not vengeance. It is a fact that evil only magnifies evil, and that, therefore, vengeance only serves more destruction. When you retaliate against other wrong doers you add fuel to the fire of destruction. But when you seek justice without retaliation then you extinguish the fire of destruction with the water of compassion. When you feel upset after you have been subjected to evil by someone let your intellect be your master and do not be carried away by emotions. In balance of what is right and what is wrong it is always the principle of an inhuman law that a human being serves. Those who act on the inhuman law of the jungle permit vengeance, but those who act on the inhuman law of the dove prohibit vengeance. Justice can never be served by vengeance, for vengeance is the violent pulse of the jungle law heart. When the option to leave a challenge is denied one can be tempted to fight back, and here is where vengeance catches root in the heart of a man. Dear friends, do not ever let the seed of vengeance catch roots within you. If you wish to live in peace you must kill the seed of vengeance before it grows and take over your mind. The seeds of the jungle law can only catch roots if you provide them with the chance and climates to grow. Therefore, when bitterness and anger overflows you, find another channel through which to release them until you experience purification. The circle of evil is like a vortex that sucks everyone around it. Watch out for the madness of war, and for the vortex of evil, for who knows what the consequences might be. Friends, without getting into specific cases I wish to stress here that this is the divine guidance in regard to justice. From the perspective of divine law, as a matter of fact, when we retaliate, or fight back, or even defend ourselves with a tinge of content, we are guilty of breaking divine law. Remove the motive of vengeance entirely from your hearts and cleanse yourselves from judgment. Justice has got nothing to do with revenge in principle. When we take pleasure in punishing others, or in retaliating against others, then we are guilty of sowing the seed of vengeance, which is the seed of war, within us. Dear doves, be careful when you are pushed to your limits, for vengeance is just a temptation. It is extremely difficult to resist the temptation of vengeance when one is loyal to justice, but if you wish not to undermine justice then get rid of the seed of vengeance. Remember, justice is not cruel, justice is compassionate, and therefore it does not welcome vengeance. Neither does justice serve vengeance nor does that vengeance serve justice. Adversely, justice and compassion serve each other and complete each other. Forgiveness is the enforcer of justice not vengeance. Justice should be served; aye justice should prevail, but only through actions which are in accordance with divine law. Here the system of man has the duty to protect an individual in cases of harassments, exploitations, and discriminations, and if it fails to do so, you should seek the help of reasonable and sensible members of society, like artists, poets, and other humanists. However, do not ever take revenge for the sake of justice. If you wish to serve justice then you must follow its source which is salvation. Follow the principles of love, peace, fairness, tolerance, patience, mercy, forgiveness, and harmony.

Comments:


When I wrote this message down I could not help thinking about the bigoted and destructive old law of the bible. Vengeance is not the law of God. Vengeance is the law of primitive men whom claimed that it was the law of God. Eye for an eye and tooth for a tooth is the law of the jungle. Vengeance does not make the offset of justice, nor does vengeance serve equality. Vengeance only serves war, and it is, in fact, the illusion of justice. Just as anarchy is the illusion of freedom so is vengeance the illusion of justice. Vengeance may look like a fish, but it is a venomous snake. Do not feed vengeance and do not touch it. Flee from vengeance like you flee from the plague. Remember, eye for an eye and tooth for a tooth is against divine law. The Old Testament's primitive law has already been abolished and subsequently usurped by divine law. I should note here, however, that this emanation is the general view and guidance of divine law, and that it has got nothing to do with pragmatism. There are exceptions related to crime and psychopathic criminals which have been expressed in many American films and television series. It is not my purpose to confound anyone, nor is it my intention to undermine my own emanation here due to the inevitability of pragmatism, but we must always bear in mind that divine statute law is embedded with the flexibility of exceptions to the balance of the physical reality. On many personal an account in Denmark I was tested and pushed to limits which I believe to be acquitted had I reacted on the pulse of vengeance and committed a crime. However, it was a test of faith, in which I have not failed, apart for some paltry cases which included protests, diatribes, and damage to property. In Denmark the individual is pushed over the edge, and driven to the extremes of crime both by the authorities and by the welfare system. The Danish rabble adds insult to injury when the victim expresses pain and/or a cry for help. Any signs of humanism are attracting bullies like magnet. Although it is easier said than done,

I have finally resisted the temptation to join the jungle law. My rebellion against inequality in society promoted justice. Since I am a follower of justice I did not use force when I was tempted to retaliate. Owing to my devotion to justice I walked through love and peace and ignored those who provoked me. In Denmark, provocation is a ritual of violence that is practiced in all sectors of society in order to preserve the predominant jungle law; thus, one encounters with endless of invitations to commit a crime on a daily basis. The animalistic commoners (hunters) are often chanting the jungle law as if they are interconnected to a demonic super organism. I remember many cases in which I was harassed, also in the jewelry shop, but also on other occasions. Here I felt the rage of the oppressed in Denmark on my own soul and body. Moreover, the individual in Denmark is often prodded to leave Denmark when one is seeking fairness and equality, justice and moral order. In cases of self defense the individual is demonized and furthermore depicted as vengeful, evil, and dangerous. The option to stay in Denmark and suffer systematic insults, oppressions, and provocations, is given to all individuals by the primitive spirit of the jungle law. When it was clear to me that it is when one defends oneself that one is condemned by society, and not when one is provoking, I did not bother to seek justice in Denmark, for it would be equal to throwing pearls to swine. The systematic provocations in Denmark are part of the systematic order to subdue the mass population to the rule of the Jante Law. I believe that I was inspired to write this emanation shortly after I was attacked by a racist ruffian in a camping place. Here I was banished from the camping area together with my two daughters (3 and 7) by the racist manager because I was a foreigner. My complaint has been dismissed because of my social status. However, I have also been subjected to endless of insults by civil servants during my unemployment, and by customers during nearly two decades of work in the jewelry shop. In Denmark vengeance is on the menu every single day because crime is enforced by the conformers, worshippers, and leaders of Danish society. In my humble view, provocation that tempts one to commit a crime is far worse than vengeance, but both vengeance and provocation are serving the jungle law in different degrees on both sides of the equation. I believe that Denmark was probably the most sophisticated evil society on earth, because the spiritual war was aptly and subtly concealed to a degree of oblivion. However, the psychological madness of Danish society is now revealed to a very large extent, not only by me, but by a new generation of foreigners who do not yield to oppression. I am proud of all rebels who did not commit a crime, but dared to voice their criticism against the evil system in Denmark. Criticizing society was a crime at the time, thus, I was proudly tagged as an offender of the jungle law. My books about the new revolution made me in fact the biggest offender of the jungle law in Denmark. However, I should mention that anyone who resorts to petty crime, which is different than criticism and art, in fact joins the jungle law. In order to break the jungle law one has to remain loyal to divine law. Criticism and art are loyal servants and efficient tools of divine law.

## Emanation XIX:    Mother Earth

Once there was a very beautiful virgin. She was happy and she lived in equilibrium and in perfect harmony with everyone. But one day the beautiful virgin was forced to get married because she had no mind of her own. However, her husband grew weary of living in peace and harmony. Thus, he began drinking alcohol and gambling. Then he was beating up his wife, abusing her, exploiting her, until he destroyed her. In such a case of disorder we ask ourselves, 'does she not deserve a decent husband instead of the primitive black hearted one that she was forced to marry?' Anyone with love and compassion in his heart, and anyone with a sense of justice will agree that the decent wife does not deserve to be mistreated, and that she deserves, instead, to be happy, and to marry a new husband. Dear friends, this is the story of mother earth. Her marriage with mankind was forced on her; though not against her will because the earth has got no will of its own. Then humankind waged war against the earth and against itself, and ever since the dawn of mankind the earth has experienced destruction. The delicate balance of the earth's eco system has been broken. The beauty and magic of millions of years has been invaded and destroyed in a short span of time. Mankind is an abusive husband, and therefore the earth is crying out for redemption. The earth is longing for a healthy relationship with mankind. The earth is yearning to be healed and restored to its original beauty. Since the earth is equated with an abused wife we ask the same questions here about the concern of mother earth. Does the earth not deserve that a prince will marry her instead of a ruffian. The earth is majestic and royal; she is a princess that deserves a prince instead of her contemporary abusive bully husband. Dear friends, the prince is the new generation of children on earth; the spirit of the new dawn, aye the spirit of salvation. The new generations of children of light are analogous to the prince of salvation. They will respect mother earth and treat her with dignity.

Moreover, they will heal the earth and not kill her. They will build her, not destroy her. This will be the marriage of equality and true love. The earth was a damsel in distress, as she lived under the tyranny of her bully husband who has exploited and abused her endlessly. But then a prince came along and saved her. He defended her and fought against her evil husband. The prince of salvation defeated the earth's bully husband and that was the end of the jungle law. Then the earth had a mind of her own and she loved her new husband. They have married out of mutual consent which was based on fairness, equality, love, and peace.

Comments:

When I wrote this parable I thought about this contemporary primitive generation on earth whose consciousness is the reflection of the jungle law. The promotion of selfishness in society removed many people from the collective responsibility to protect the earth. However, before the earth can marry the prince of salvation she needs to get a divorce from her bully husband. It means that there has to be a global revolution in which the jungle law will be toppled down. Thereupon, divine law will be restored and affect the spirit of the age until the earth will be healed. Our planet earth is a beautiful decent woman. Therefore every person chooses whether to be the earth's rapist or the earth's prince of salvation. I should remark here that the weak in a human society is analogous to the earth. When we follow the jungle law the weak in a human society is abused, but when we follow divine law then the weak in society is treated with respect. Equality is the measure of fairness, for the balance of the earth's beauty is in fact the virtue of equality.

Emanation XX:     Divine senses


Dear friends, apart from our physical senses we are also blessed with spiritual senses which are associated with the two inhuman, yet dynamic properties of Yin and Yang. It is owing to our creed and faith that we choose which spiritual senses to develop and which spiritual senses to eradicate. Our spiritual evolution allows us to choose a development between dove's wings and hyena's jaws. The followers of the jungle law develop primitive, predatory, and reptilian senses, like the sense to cheat others for money. However, the followers of divine law develop an acute sense of justice, which is a divine sense just like humor. All divine senses are healing senses. The refinement that we receive from laughter, thanks to a comedian, is similar to the refinement that we receive from cases of law in which justice prevail. Therefore I urge you, dear doves, always to sharpen your divine senses and evolve in the spirit accordingly. Justice is a sense which is serving the balance of ethics. The moral sphere is the most important sphere, as it is the way to salvation. A human being is associated with the zero paradox and therefore many people claim that justice does not really exist. But justice is like a human being; it does exist. Owing to faith justice exists. However, divine senses are like trees, they need water, sunlight, nourishment, good soil, and a lot of tender loving care. Sense of humor and sense of justice are interconnected, just like the senses of compassion and sense of reason. The sense of morals and the sense of reason are chief divine senses in all human beings and in all human societies. Thus, without the divine senses a man is bound to live in a very dark and primitive consciousness. A human society which does not promote divine senses is bound to live in the darkness of the middle ages. Friends, artists are blessed with the divine sense of creativity. Humanists are blessed with the divine sense of morals. Altruists are blessed with the divine senses of generosity and charity. Dear friends: grace is also a divine sense and a divine virtue. Grace is the source of inner beauty, therefore I urge to grow with divine law and develop your divine senses. A man who lives his life by the divine senses is a man that has found the Garden of Eden. The way to salvation is through the air and through the sky, not through the caves and not through the ground. Hence, divine senses are analogous to wings of birds. The way to Paradise is through the sky. Dear doves; develop your wings and fly away up high in the sky. Then you can land on the tree of life, and flit from the tree of life to the tree of knowledge and vice versa. The search for salvation begins with the development of the divine senses. Humor is a healer, justice is a redeemer. Friends, without the divine senses our existence on earth is obsolete and insignificant. Therefore, I urge you to rebel against the jungle law and to eradicate all beastly senses. Do not ever develop beaks and talons like the predatory opportunists, for they hunt for money and material comfort, and their ways are dark and subterranean. The predatory limbs of inequality confine one to darkness and war, but the limbs that evolve from equality liberate one from darkness and war. The limbs that evolve from equality are the wings of the dove of peace that leads to total freedom. Dear doves, if you wish to find heaven within yourselves, please follow peace and its divine senses. The reward of the altruist is the nectar of equality, but the reward of the selfish is the decay of inequality. Dear doves, we feed on grains of wheat, not on flesh and blood. Therefore I urge you to work hard on the development of the divine senses until you feel that your wings are strong enough to fly towards the trees of paradise.

Comments:

This inspiration, I believe, will open the mind of the reader to the dangers of the jungle law. Swindlers, whom cheat others systematically for money, are still considered heroes in many human societies. Such swindlers drink the wine of selfishness and madness with which society provides them. Such swindlers have developed a keen sense to cheat others without getting caught. When there is no decency, equality, or peace within society then many folks get a free way to develop their jungle law senses. The state of the collective mind is ill, because often decent folks are oppressed whereas corrupt folks are praised in society. However, the revolution begins with the self. Hence, those who are wise will develop their divine senses and evolve with their spiritual gifts, whereas those whom are engrossed with ignorance cannot find progress because of their moral deficiency and because divine senses have not evolved within them. Balance is also a divine sense; hence we often encounter a pattern in which the jungle law follower is always frustrated and angry, whereas the divine law follower is always harmonious and serene. One has to delve deep in order to realize the truth about one's own evolution. When I started to write poetry in a frantic manner, back in 1995, I had no clue that I was in fact evolving owing to the divine sense of creativity. The more I channeled and the more I embraced my spiritual gift, then the faster and stronger that my wings were developed. It was a very long journey for me in exile. It was an epic journey that rewarded me in spirit but destroyed me in body. The ill-willing physical reality through which I had to emerge was mentally unbearable. Thus, it was owing to the divine senses of humor, justice, and creativity that I have managed to fly above the inferno of Danish society.

## Emanation XXI:    A spiritual Bigamy

Greetings, friends; peace and love upon you on the behalf of the divine order. Imagine salvation and vanity as two brides. Each man chooses his bride in accordance with his faith. According to the law of man it happens that a man is not allowed to marry two women, for such an act is a felony known as bigamy. It is the same with the spiritual world. A man cannot follow both war and peace. Either that a man believes in peace, or that he believes in war. It is the same in regard to equality and inequality, for no man on earth can serve both equality and inequality. Any man who serves the jungle law and divine law at the same time is equal to a double agent spy, or to a man who is charged with bigamy. Therefore, we should make it clear to ourselves that we follow divine law only, and that our bride is spiritual freedom, salvation. Either one marries salvation or that one marries vanity, but a man should not even attempt to marry them both. Salvation and vanity are two fierce opposites, which are similar to two parallel lines that never meet and never cross. Therefore, I urge you to get rid of all the vanities to which you are attached in the material world. Get rid of your love of Mammon. Get rid of your infatuation with material comfort. Get rid of your obsession with vain pride. Rebel against nationalism and religion, and rebel against the jungle law! Divorce vanity, for she is a rotten evil wife. Divorce her before she will destroy you and collect your inheritance. Vanity is a gold digger whose only intention is to consume you until you are dead. Dear friends, if you are married to vanity, rest assured that you have already dug up your own grave. Hence, it is only a matter of time before vanity hammers down the last nail in your coffin. Dear doves, if you wish to have a happy long life, then you should marry the bride of heaven, salvation. When a man is divorced from vanity, he has then a chance to court and woo a beautiful bride called salvation. It might take a long time before a man could find her. Because salvation is as rare as she is beautiful, and she is hard to find. But when a man finds her it might take long time to woo her. But when the magic happens then she might agree to marry the decent humble man. Dear friends, this is how the world will be shifted from the jungle law to divine law; from a dark age to an age of light and truth. This is how mankind will be able to attain spiritual freedom. However, first of all, mankind needs to divorce vanity; she is the old ugly harpy wife whom he married in the madness of war. Vanity is the bride of spiritual death, thus, anyone who signs contracts with her is doomed for self destruction. But anyone who marries salvation is bound to find nirvana and an everlasting spiritual life. The taste of the lips of vanity is bitter because of her madness and power, but the taste of the lips of salvation is sweet because of her love and beauty. Do not ever kiss with vanity, because she will render you with the deadly kiss of hell. Kiss with salvation, for she will render you with the divine kiss of heaven. Once you have tasted the sweet kiss of salvation, and you'd be cured from all the maladies of vanity.

Comments:

This emanation reminded me about the book 'The balance of justice' because of the double life of a human being due to the paradox of existence. However, I should remark here that although we are married to both vanity and salvation because of the shackles of the two dynamic forces, we can still choose a bride. We are in fact compelled to choose a path in life, either forwards or backwards, either good or evil, either divine or primitive. My personal marriage with the heavenly bride Shira (Poetry), who is a daughter of salvation, supplied me with the blessings of salvation. As for my marriage with an earthling woman, I have experienced the complete opposite of happiness. In that sense I lived happily in the metaphysical dimension because of my poetry, but in the physical world I have been unhappy all of my life. In that sense, my heavenly bride was salvation whereas my humanoid wife was vanity. Vanity wanted me to dispose of my heavenly bride salvation, because she felt that salvation was posing a threat on her mad reality. Salvation, on the other hand, did not want me to be lonely in the world of man, and therefore she thought that I should find a woman on earth. The conflicts between the realities pushed me to the boundary of insanity, and often I was detached from the physical reality due to depressions and pangs. Moreover, my opinion about marriage has changed dramatically after I became a victim of such a vain ritual on earth. In my humble view, marriage shouldn't be involved with the law of man. Marriage in a way is a tyrant, because it violates the freedom of the individual to live in peace of mind. The old law of the bible is at fault because no human being is born to suffer the nonsense of a human society. A man should be always free in spirit, free at heart, and free in mind. The primitive law that suggests 'Until death will do you part' is in fact a dictation from the jungle law. Indeed it is a primitive chant and a primitive ritual. In adverse to marriage, it is love, happiness, and truth that should prevail in all relationships, not power, fear, and lies. Human society is very narrow minded in regard to happiness, because marriage is prioritized on the account of fairness and truth. Like equality, happiness cannot be systemized. This book was a pleasure for me to write. Furthermore, I hope mankind will survive the transitional period of the new age and move to a higher level of consciousness as soon as the jungle law will become notorious instead of trendy. All in all, this book covered many important messages which I wrote in the spiritual desert of exile. My sufferings, I believe, will reward others in the future. In Denmark I was the man who was stung by wasps every single day for nearly two decades. However, the honey which I extracted inside the flowers of my soul is now served to mankind from the secret hive of heaven. Peace.

Printed in Great Britain
by Amazon.co.uk, Ltd.,
Marston Gate.